GOD-FLAVORS AND GOD-COLORS
Reflections on the
Sermon on the Mount

R. PAGE SHELTON, Doctor of Ministry

GOD-FLAVORS AND GOD-COLORS
Reflections on the Sermon on the Mount

ISBN-13: 978-1720810186
ISBN-10: 1720810184

TABLE OF CONTENTS

PART II: MATTHEW 6

PART III: MATTHEW 7

Dedication

**This book is dedicated to my wife
Jann Briscoe
for her encouragement and for sharing
her spiritual journey as a guide and
loving partner.**

Explanation of Special Word Usage

I. <u>Pronoun references to God</u>: An ongoing debate among writers today concerns whether to refer to God as *He* or *She*. God is referred to primarily as male. However, there are references to God as female in Genesis, the Psalms, and the Prophets. I alternate by paragraphs the use of the masculine and feminine pronouns to refer to God.

II. <u>Sin and sins</u>: In Romans 7 Paul's discussion includes a cosmic Sin that is capitalized. This ties for me the discussion of principalities and powers in Ephesians 6. Cosmic Sin describes for me the cosmic evil that competes with God to control the universe. I understand cosmic Sin as being the tempter of Jesus after his 40 days in the wilderness. I have chosen to refer to cosmic Sin with a capital S.

Sin with a lower case "s" refers to the offenses we commit. These include lying, cheating, blaming, speaking half-truths, violence, and other actions that are destructive or intentionally chaotic. These are usually committed against other people. They are a rejection of God's way love and mercy. They also create a barrier between God and us.

ABOUT THIS BOOK – AN INTRODUCTION

I

When I read an introduction to a book, I wonder what has influenced an author's heart and mind to write that particular book. I decided to share with you some of the influences in recent years that have influenced my writing this book.

I write to open my heart and mind to what God is saying. Primarily, I focus on scripture passages. I sought to hear Gods' Word through the written words of scripture. This was a form of *Lectio Divina*.

For those who may not know, *Lectio Divina* is an ancient Christian practice of using scripture passages to pray. This approach to prayer is to let the Spirit focus our hearts and minds on a word, phrase, or longer parts of a passage of scripture. We let the Spirit guide us to focus what God is saying to us today in the scripture we are reading. It involves a lot of silence and listening through the Spirit with our hearts.

This is what writing on passages of scripture does for me. I hear different meaning for my life from God each time I read a passage. This indicates to me that I need a different word from God for different times in my life. The Spirit enables me to hear a deeper meaning of living God's love and mercy.

II

Have you ever thought of not simply being part of God's human creation, but part of the entire universe? The mystics from the 4th century realized this. Modern science is discovering that a dynamic force holds the universe together. This new awakening has helped me understand better what Paul is saying in Romans 8:19 that the whole cosmos is waiting for humans to be redeemed and living in God's love alone.

It is amazing to think about being connected with the furthest galaxy and smallest particles in space. One writer says that our prayers and how we live the Christian life also affects the universe.

III

During my last 20+ years, the way of the Contemplative Life has had the most influence in my life. The writers of this way awaken me to understanding the scriptures as telling of the love and mercy of God to me. The Spirit is leading me through ways of living the Contemplative Life to realize the amazing joy of knowing piece by piece the centrality of the loving relationship with God that comes through surrendering my will to Him through the lifelong work of the Spirit.

I will not attempt to describe the way of the Contemplative Life. There are many books on the Contemplative Life written by men and women who are more capable than I am to help you understand how this practice draws toward an intimate relationship with God. They have lived the Contemplative way in God's love much longer and deeper than I have.

Thomas Merton, a contemporary mystic who died in the 1960s, says that contemplation is going through a desert wilderness without food, water, or shelter on the way to the promised land in unity with God and living the true self in love that She created for us to be one with Her and all people. Writing helps me follow the Spirit along the desert path to the promised land of living more my true self.

Only the Spirit can lead me through this desert to the place where I can discover who God created me to be. The Spirit gives us brothers and sisters in Christ with whom we share the journey. The Spirit also keeps us in touch with the cloud of witnesses who have gone before us.

This wilderness is made up of habits of my little self-centered ego. My little ego is important early in life, as I learn at church and home the information that tells me the rules to follow to live the Christian life. However, there comes a time when the ways of the little ego are not adequate to give guidance to living daily God's love and mercy, especially as we grow older and our life experiences broaden our understanding of faith and relationship with God and the universe.

The Spirit shows us how our little ego works against God's love and purpose. The little ego leads us to be concerned with personal wants and expectations. It focuses on our personal self-interests rather than God's way of life.

I am grateful for the Spirit being with me through the desert and encouraging me each day to ways that draw me into ever deeper relationship with God. Through the Spirit I am learning to depend on Her love to enable me to love myself. I am awed by the difference in my life such loving makes in my relationships with Her, others, and me. It is truly a transformative awakening.

IV

I felt led to write again on the Sermon on the Mount, but differently from my other book titled: SALT AND LIGHT. The Spirit gave me the desire to reflect on the Sermon in light of God's love and mercy.

I believed that too much of my first book on the Sermon came out of disappointments and hurts that I experienced in the churches I grew up in, served, or attended. I am sure that many in the churches were disappointed in me at the time.

The Spirit has led me to understand that the Sermon is about a life of God's love and not as a basis for criticizing others. The Sermon speaks of how individuals and the church as the body of Christ live a counterculture life to modern culture and society

The discernment about the focus of this book came in December 2014. This was after exploring different approaches for the previous 3 or 4 years.

After a year and a half working on the book the Spirit has awakened me to God's love. This has changed everything for me. I am experiencing myself as loveable and becoming more awake to God's love in the midst of relationships, which has changed my sense of relating to others. God's love is different from any I have known.

My journey is also leading me through painful experiences of letting go of my egocentric love from the past in order to let God's love embrace me and transform me.

Our little ego ways are the ones we know best. The Spirit is leading us through the unknown land of God's love so that we may love as we are loved.

V

In JESUS CHRIST SUPERSTAR Mary Magdalene sings "Don't Know How to Love Him." She is describing her struggles with being in love with Jesus and how different is his love from all other men.

She both desires his love and is fearful of it because it is different from any she has experienced. This song describes a lot of how I was feeling at the time the Spirit was inviting me to a journey into a deeper experience of God's love.

In reminding me of this song the Spirit reminded me of some biblical passages on love that I have found important. The passages are:

Matthew 22:36-37: "Love the Lord your God with all your passion and prayer and intelligence." The second part of the commandment is "love others as well as you love yourself." All of God's laws and commands are understood by this command.

I John 4:16: "We know it so well, we've embraced it heart and soul, this love that comes from God. God is love. When we take up permanent residence in a life of love, we live in God and God lives in us." God does not simply love. He is love itself.

John 13:34-35: "Let me give you a new command: Love one another. In the same way I loved you, you love one another. This is how everyone will recognize that you are my disciples—when they see the love you have for each other." The love we know from God through Christ is the love we are to share with one another as brothers and sisters in Christ.

The Spirit also reminds me of how Romans 13:10, Ephesians 1:4, Galatians 5:22, and I Corinthians 13 are additional guides in my journey.

VI

Another recent influence in my journey is St. Therese of Lisieux. The Spirit led me to her autobiography, THE STORY OF A SOUL, and a book that interprets her life and teachings, WALKING THE LITTLE WAY OF THERESE OF LISIEUX by Joseph F. Schmidt, FSC. She lived based on God's love at a time when the church was emphasizing perfection as the proper spiritual life.

Several of her reflections that give light to my journey are:

1. She opened her heart to live with God in love that healed her hurts and transformed her relationships.
2. She recognized her imperfections and experienced God's loving her in them.
3. Her emotions often got in the way of receiving God's transforming love.
4. Love does not include verbal or physical violence to others or to herself.
5. Love is accepting the imperfections of others and of herself.
6. Love of God requires giving her willingness to do His will.
7. Love of God means sharing this love with others that they may also love God.

VII

I am grateful for my community of love with whom I experience being supported, sustained, forgiven, and reconciled. I am especially grateful for the mercy of God in all the times I fail to act or speak in His love. I am awakening to the important of brothers and sisters in Christ in knowing God's love and mercy

I appreciate your joining my journey as you read these reflections. Let us open our hearts to God's blessings and desire to live with us in transforming love of heart and mind.

VIII

This book describes my understanding so far of how I am to live the Christian Life that Jesus teaches in the Sermon on the Mount. I wrote the book as a way to clarify for myself what I read in the Sermon.

I told some friends a little of what I was discovering through the Spirit in the Sermon. They told me that I should share my writing with others. It was my intent for this to be a personal work. As I listened to the Spirit, I concluded that I could share what the Spirit has clarified for me. What I have learned, the Spirit may use for others.

The Sermon is divided into passages that I have placed in separate chapters. The reflections are a few pages in length. The focus is the Christian life based on God's love and mercy. As I wrote, the Spirit opened the eyes of my heart the differences the Christian life is described in the Sermon than I have read in previous studies of the Sermon and the way people make the Sermon less radical.

Page Shelton, 2018

PART 1: MATTHEW 5

Chapter 1: Less of You; More of God

"You're blessed when you're at the end of your rope. With less of you there is more of God and his rule." (5:3)

What does it mean to be at the end of your rope? It usually refers to having a life crisis that we have no solution for. We have reached the point of seeing no alternative solution and needing help. The other question we want to explore is what Jesus could have meant when he says, 'with less of you there is more of God and his rule.'

I think of times when I felt as if I had reached the end of my rope. I usually panic first because I am not sure what will happen. Once I wondered whether I would survive the crisis. What I did was to remember if I could find a solution to the problem. Reaching the end of my rope focused my efforts on what I could do to survive the crisis.

Most of my life I relied on myself to solve problems. That is the way I was taught growing up: I was in charge of my life and had to solve my problems alone. So, I preferred not having crises. I worked hard to anticipate problems and prevent them from happening. I never thought of crises as blessings or of how God would be involved with them.

I heard in Divinity School the term of "god of the gap." This is what many of us believe is God's expectation. We exhaust our abilities and then call on God to bridge the gap between the crisis and the solution. Jesus says God is not interested in filling the gap, but in filling our hearts.

I believe Jesus is telling us that we are blessed when crises in our lives empty our minds and hearts of our little controlling ego ways of dealing with a crisis. We fill our hearts and minds with our success and do not see how God was involved.

We are blessed when we stop relying on ourselves. Then we have more room in our hearts for God's love and mercy to solve our problems based on our faith and trust in His love and mercy. These are the ways that lead us to surrender our wills to God through the guidance of the Spirit. Then we become willing to open our hearts and mind to God ways.

The Contemplative life helped me see, how I was living out the "god of the gap." Approach. I was not letting the Spirit fill my life with God's way of living. I became more aware that God blessed me with the crisis in order for the Spirit to lead me into receiving God's love and mercy in my heart.

I know that I have not fully surrendered to God when I still try to solve my crisis without centering my prayers on God's presence and love. It is still a new notion that God knows better what is right for me than I do or anyone else does. When I remember, I wait in silence for the work of God's Spirit in my heart.

Desiring to hear in my heart God's word means that I am letting the Spirit clean out more of my little ego from my heart and mind that says I can handle the crisis and do not need God getting in the way. However, by recognizing my need for God, I let the Spirit fill my heart with God rather than with my inadequate solutions. When I open my heart to the Spirit, the Spirit makes more room in my heart for God's loving and righteous will.

The Spirit leads me to know in my heart that only God can lead me to find a way to live through a crisis to know Her peace in my heart and mind. Then I know that God is with me at the end of the rope and will be with me regardless what happens.

I must remember that I may suffer through some crises. God gives us no guarantees that He will solve all crises for us. What is important is that we let the Spirit fill our hearts with God's love that we may rely on God in all situations.

I learn from the Spirit as I go along life's way what it means to give more room to God and less room for my wants and expectations. The blessing becomes an increase in faith and trust in God.

The Sermon is about living God's kingdom of love individually and as the body of Christ. It is about how we live with more of Him and less of us. It is about putting into practice daily at home, at work, socially, and in church the truth of His love. We can do this only as individuals and as a church. We give God more and more room in our hearts.

Matthew may have placed this verse intentionally at the beginning of the Sermon on the Mount. As I worked through the Sermon, I observed that everything Jesus teaches in the Sermon relates back to this Beatitude.

The Sermon is filled with difficult ways of living the Christian life. We often struggle to let the Spirit lead us to live the Christian life taught in the Sermon. It is also difficult to let go of what we have learned in the world that is counter to what Jesus teaches in the Sermon.

More room for God means that I do less to live my life based on self-interests and self-concerns. I spend more time letting Her fill my life with Her concerns and relying on Her for my needs. I let the Spirit fill my heart with faith in the love and mercy of God.

Faith is not primarily about beliefs or good works. Faith is about a way of life that gives the most room in our hearts to God that we may live the way of His love, mercy, and justice. It is what fills our hearts with more of God than of ourselves.

A Blessing

We are here to let the Spirit guide us into living God's love in all aspects of our lives. We are here to have our lives transformed and filled with Him and His presence, rather than with our personal demands and wants.

A Prayer

Loving God, I desire that you occupy more and more the rooms of my heart.

Chapter 2: Embraced by the One Dearest

"You're blessed when you feel you've lost what is most dear to you. Only then can you be embraced by the One most dear to you." (5:4)

What blessing is there when death or moving far away separates us from people we hold most dear in our hearts? My experience is that there is a lot of tears and sadness. Some people feel lost. Others want to know why this person was taken from them.

We have family and friends who are dear to our hearts. We feel a connection with them that has no words, except that we love them. We feel as if we are a part of them.

They are the ones who understand us better than we understand ourselves. They can say the word or words our hearts need to hear in times of confusion or doubt. They speak the word we need to hear when we are troubled in our hearts but cannot say what the trouble is.

They are the ones who come to sit with us in silence when we need comfort and the presence of one we love with all out heart. They know words are desired or helpful at certain times. They know that a presence and a touch say all that we need to hear and can tolerate to receive.

We do the same for them. We are as dear to them as they are to us. When we are together we feel oneness and love that cannot be explained. When we part there is sadness, but we know that we are never separated from them in our hearts.

We are likely to lose the one dear to our hearts at some point. We lose them most permanently through death. We do not have them to see each day or when we want to. We do not experience the presence of their understanding our hearts nor our understanding their hearts. We may not physically sit with them to share our hearts and souls, but we still feel the closeness.

They still retain a special place in our hearts. We think of them. We remember conversations as if they were present beside us. However, it is different not to have them with us. We feel some emptiness not having someone who understands as well or better than we do.

We may also lose someone by changes in life. Our most dear one and we may drift apart for whatever reason. The time with them is still special and life changing for us. Yet, that time may be temporary, even as it was special.

To have someone on earth as most dear to us may affect our relationship with God. Even if we take time to open our heart to be close to God, our human natures may give most of our heart to our loved one on earth, since we can touch them, converse with them in person, and experience knowing and being known by them in heart and mind.

I can imagine someone saying that the earthly relationship described above is a gift from God. That is true. The difficulty is that the people dearest to each other may forget this or may not recognize God's presence making them dearest to each other.

Jesus says that when we no longer have someone most dear to us dominating our heart, our hearts are more open to be filled with the one who does know us best. We come to know God heart to heart. This open our heart to deeper love for the earthly one most dear to us.

What makes God most dear to us? Jesus describes this in the Sermon. God loves us better than our family or friends. God knows us better than we know ourselves or even than our earthly loved ones know us.

God enables us to know more deeply our relationship we have with Her. God knows what is right for us. She knows that our love for Her is to be reflected in our love for our earthly loved ones and that our love for earthly loved ones reflects our love for Her.

God gives us the Spirit to transform our lives that we may love others and ourselves with Her love. She awakens us to the person She created us to be. She enables us to live with others in Her love and mercy.

God gives us people on earth to love dearly. We know each other deeply through God's love that fills our heart through the Spirit. No greater gift comes from God than His love that we receive and give to others.

The gift of a dear one is not for our personal benefit alone, even though that happens. God gives us dear ones that we may know in a small way the relationship we can have with Her. This is seen where 2 or 3 dear ones on earth gather in Christ's name to live the way and truth of Christ.

To love God more than anyone on earth enables us to be embraced by Him. When Israel was in exile and returned to their land, Isaiah 61:3 tells us that He embraced them to give them hearts of joy:

> "To care for the needs of all who mourn in
> Zion,
> give them bouquets of roses instead of
> ashes
> Messages of joy instead of news of doom,
> a praising heart instead of a languid
> spirit.
> Rename them 'Oaks of Righteousness"
> planted by God to display his glory.

A Blessing

We are here to live in God's love as the dearest love we can experience. We are here to have deep relationships with earthly dear ones, as we have with God.

A Prayer

I desire, O God, for you to hold me in comfort as the one I love most dearly.

Chapter 3: Content with Who You Are

"You're blessed when you're content with just who you are — no more, no less. That's the moment you find yourself proud owners of everything that can't be bought." (5:5)

Are you content with who you are? You may know people who are not content with themselves. They may be taking self-improvement courses. They may complain about their looks and try to improve themselves to look prettier or more handsome. They spend time working hard to get a head to have more esteem from others or more money for a better car or larger house.

Some people wish that they were prettier or more handsome? They may wish that they had more money or more influence? Some feel lonely at times and wished that you had someone to share a more heart to heart relationship?

On the other hand, you may not think about being different than you are. You may feel it is a waste of time to think about the impossible. You may get on with life or find a way to escape. You may not bother with thinking about being content or not, but you are who you are, and other people will have to be content with that.

Might Jesus mean something like I've said above? What might he mean by saying that being content with the way I am is a blessing?

I have known a few people who are content with who they are. They have decided that they are the way they are, and they would live the best they could. Some even say that they are the way God made them and they would do their best to live for God.

The message I had received from the church when growing up was that I was supposed to be perfect. I was to live God's laws and the moral teachings of the church perfectly. I believed this and tried to live this way.

The reality I learned, as I became an adult, was that no one could ever be perfect regardless how hard they tried. Yet, perfection was all I knew as a standard for judging whether I was content with myself. I assumed God and others use the same standard. I assumed that not being perfect meant that God is not content with me.

I also assumed that contentment came from how satisfied people were with my actions. I assumed that such acceptance from others let me accept myself. I assumed that if others were content with me that I could stop trying so hard to be perfect.

In my later years I began to read the writers who described the Contemplative Life. They gave me a different perspective on being content. These mystics of the church found that contentment comes for God's love and mercy. Contentment comes from living in that love daily. It meant letting the Spirit transform my heart from trying to be perfect to being filled with God's love and mercy.

I discovered that something was missing to make me content with my life. God had wonderfully made me, and I kept messing it up by trying to be content with being perfect. I kept trying to find contentment in my job, my house, or the esteem of others. I knew that these things did not make me content with myself.

So, what am I to do to be content with myself? What must I do to stop trying to be content with money or esteem of others?

Until the first of August 2016 I would not have understood how this Beatitude applies to my life. I knew that I was not content with how I saw myself. I realized that I am worth loving by others and by me. On that day I heard God say in my heart that I should get to know the Page He had created, because Page is a loveable person. I learned that I had to open my heart to the presence of God. This meant surrendering all my efforts at cultural or perfect contentment

It meant that I had to desire for the Spirit to transform me from contentment by the standards of this world to contentment by God's love and mercy.

I knew that I could not do this alone. I had tried, and my efforts were just too inadequate to enable me to live God's love and mercy each day. There are people that I find very difficult to love, much less like. Yet, they are God's children also and I am to respect that. I needed help to be wise enough to love others without putting myself in dangerous situations or make dangerous enemies.

I discovered that Centering Prayer is important in my learning to love and to be content. The men and women practicing the Contemplative Life talked about Centering Prayer as an important way for the Spirit to open me up to God's love.

I learned through reading and experience that this means establishing a daily practice of Centering Prayer to let the Spirit guide my life and transform my heart. It is not easy to sit in silence for 20 minutes (although I started out with 10 minutes and worked up to 20 minutes). It is not easy to let the thoughts pass through the mind boats or objects on a flowing river without examining them or dwelling on them.

It is an amazing experience done over years. I believe that this practice of opening to God let me one day say that I don't have to keep being perfect and doing everything right. I began to find a loveable Page within me. The more I find contentment with myself and the more I give myself permission to be imperfect and to fail. It took me several years to have a daily practice of Centering Prayer.

I read a story about a person from outside a monastery asking a monk what they did in the monastery. He said that they repeatedly fall down and get up. This metaphor is that they constantly fail—i.e., fall down. They get up because the love and mercy of God gives them strength to continue to grow into the person He created them to be.

Jesus says that I am blessed when I am content with 'just who I am—no more, no less.' He says it is all right to fall down since God's Spirit always helps me get up.

Contentment occurs when the Spirit leads me to accept myself, as God accepts me. I do not need to pretend to be more competent, more knowledgeable, more perfect, or more of a success than I am. I am free to growing in the ways and love that He created me to be.

I found the beginning of lasting contentment on that first of August 2016. It was more than a surprise to receive this light in my darkness. It was a shock. I could not believe this unexpected awakening at first. The Spirit would not let me avoid this gift from God. I spent the first month with the Spirit's help awakening to some initial understanding of what this means. I talked with friends who said that they had seen my being loving and lovable as long as they had known me.

I spent time grieving over the pain that I had felt most of my life not knowing the depth and breadth of God's love. I grieved over not accepting God's love and mercy that leads me to deeper contentment. I did not like myself and was critical of others not being perfect in the way I thought that they should be. I also felt the pain that I had given to other people from a discontented heart and mind.

The Spirit is leading me into the next part of this journey to know what it is like to love myself—to be content with me as I am. I am awakening to what it is to be content with myself without imposing perfectionism. It is a joyous journey. It is difficult letting go what I have done and felt for over 70 years.

I cannot explain how this transformation happened, or where it is leading me. I may know in general but not in details. Yet, I need not understand it or explain it.

This revelation changed my life. It is what St. Therese of Lisieux caller her second conversion.

I know that the Spirit has much to transform in my life. My journey continues with consciousness on my part that there is much to know about living God's love.

Being content with myself in God cannot be bought at any price. It is a free gift. It leads me to living more peacefully and lovingly in the world. That cannot be bought at any price.

A Blessing

We are here to be content in a loving relationship with God made possible by Her love. We are here to be content that She loves us in our imperfections.

Prayer

Blessed Christ, my desire is for your Spirit to guide me to live in contentment in you, especially in your mercy and love.

.

Chapter 4: A Good Appetite for God

"You're blessed when you've worked up a good appetite for God. He's food and drink in the best meal you'll ever eat." (5:6)

I was startled when I first read this translation. I have never heard, read, or thought of an image of God as a meal. Have you?

I have never thought of God as food and drink. I have not thought of God as the best meal I would ever eat. What kind of blessing is this?

My initial thought focused on food that I eat daily. I thought about how food satisfies hunger. It is what we do to keep our bodies working properly. It is what we do to stay healthy and have energy.

When I think of an especially good meal, I think of Thanksgiving, Christmas, family reunions, or special occasions such as 50th wedding anniversaries or 90th birthdays.

When I think of working up a good appetite, I think of a day's hard labor. I think of spending a couple of hours working out at the gym. I also think of professional sports players who work hard in playing their sports.

In this Beatitude Jesus is not leading us to consider God a plate of physical food cooked just as we like it. He is not blessing us with working up appetites for a banquet table groaning with a lot of food that is God.

There is a parable about a king giving a wedding banquet. All the peers of the realm promised to attend. On the night of the banquet the peers gave many excuses to the king's servant for not attending.

The king does not let the food go to waste. He was angry with his peers refusing to attend his banquet and going back on their promise to attend. He then sent his servants to invite everyone to the banquet they see on the street, including the poor, homeless, and strangers. These marginalize people of society accepted the invitation and filled the banquet hall that the wealth and religious would not.

When the king arrives, he must be pleased that his banquet tables are full to celebrate his son's wedding. In looking around the hall, he notices that one person does not have on the proper clothes for the banquet. He asks the man how he dared to attend the banquet without wearing the proper clothes.

The king had the man thrown out. Not only thrown out but tied up and thrown into hell, which is the place without God. The king wants to be sure the man never returned to the banquet. Several has said in my hearing that this was harsh treatment.

How could anyone off the street have the right wedding clothes? They would have to come off the street in the clothes they had. Everyone but this man did have the correct wedding clothes.

I assume that the servants gave every guest a wedding garment and this man refused his, for whatever reason. It is important to realize that all things come from God and to refuse them is to refuse God.

This last paragraph of the passage gives a clue to what Jesus is saying and why Dr. Peterson translated the passage as he did. We need to remember that the story is not literal and historical. As all of the teachings of God through Jesus, this story means more that the words.

Jesus is not telling us to literally work up an appetite for a grand banquet with God as the main course. He is not saying that God is the best plate of physical food and drink that our tongues will taste, and our bodies will absorb.

Jesus is telling us to open our minds and hearts to God. He offers Himself through Christ that we receive all that we need to nourish our hearts and minds. Christ is known as the bread of life, the cup of salvation, and the water that quiches all thirst.

God is the best banquet we will ever have because God fills our lives with Her love and mercy that draws us deeper into relationship with Her. Her food gives us the spiritual strength to live according to Her love and Christ's teaching. She transforms us to live all the blessings that She gives us that the world may know the reality of Her good news.

We open our hearts to the food of His love and living word through the leading of the Spirit in prayer, the reading of God's word, and the Eucharist. We humbly and willingly accept His invitation to His banquet. We commit to give Him our total loyalty.

We let Him give us the garments we need for the banquet, rather than decide what we believe is appropriate. Even our clothes are gifts of God and not chosen by our will or to impress others.

We accept the clothing God gives us to celebrate our transformed lives through Christ. We join with brothers and sisters at Her table to partake of the best banquet we shall ever have.

The Spirit leads us to prepare ourselves to receive the nourishment we need from the food of faith, which also enables us to grow in humility to be daily the person God created us to be. The next time you eat the bread and drink the wine of the Eucharist, or Communion or Lord's Supper, be reminded that you are partaking of the best meal of God's love and mercy you will ever have.

A Blessing

We are here to feast on what God gives us for our faith and life. We are here to be nourished by Christ's bread and wine. We are here to join with brothers and sisters in Christ at the banquet given by God. We are here to eat Christ bread and hunger no more. We are here to drink Christ's wine and thirst no more.

Prayer

O God, stimulate my appetite through your Spirit that my heart and soul will be nourished and satisfied by Your love that we share with the universe.

Chapter 5: You Are Cared For

You're blessed when you care. At the moment of being 'care-full,' you find yourselves cared for." (5:7)

I know many people who are good caregivers. I've talked with people who are full of care for others, and long for an occasional giving of care to those needing care.

Some people naturally are full of care for others. Some are willing to reluctantly give care. Others give care and expect care in return from those whom they care for.

Caring for another is draining and demanding. It needs to be understood as a gift from God. The Spirit can enable all of us can show caring in a variety of ways, no matter how limited the caring or the reluctance of the caregiver.

The Christian gives care as an expression of God' love. They care for others because the other needs care and consent to be care for.

It is not part of the Christian life to have the attitude and expectation that 'I'll care for you if you will care for me.' Just as caring if a grace, gift, from God to us, our caregiving is a grace, gift, to others.

Being 'care-full' gives us a different perspective than being 'careful.' Being 'careful' focuses on doing thing that will keep us safe. Being 'care-full' changes our view from being concerned with ourselves to being concerned with taking care of others.

At my mother's memorial service all those who spoke of her said that they remember that she had a kind word for them and did what she could to help. My mother spent her life caring for others.

She was a single mother in the 1940s, which was not easy. She had a steady job. She worked hard to take of me as I was growing up. She insisted that I be kind and compassionate to all people I met.

After her second stroke, my mother felt isolated. She lost her long-term memory. She often said a different word from the one she meant. For instance, she saw some school kids and referred to their backpacks as skateboards. She could not understand all the words people said to her. She always showed that she was listening to others, even when she did not understand and could not remember the words to say in response.

My mother and I had a tense relationship most of her life. I felt that too often her caregiving of me intruded in my life.

She had two strokes within less than a year. The second one left her without long term or short-term member. Actually, she could remember some things for brief while.

I made the decision that I would do all I could to make comfortable the last part of her life. She had had a hard life, yet she had cared for others. I believed that she deserved to have comfort in her last years.

It cost me extra physical pain because of my fibromyalgia to spend time with her and to go to see her frequently. However, I was awakened to the reality that I felt cared for after I left caring for her. I was also awakened to Jesus' words of laying down your life for those you love and doing unto him what we did to others.

I had not thought of that time in this way until I read this Beatitude. I began to understand that God cared for me, as I was full of care for her.

I am not bragging about what I did. My intention is to illustrate what I hear the Jesus is saying to me.

This wasn't the only time that I felt being cared for by God. It is not the only time that I heard people tell their story about feeling cared for when they were willing to care for others with all they had.

God did not care for me because I gave my mother the care that I could. This did not feel like a reward. I felt that as I took care of God's child. God took care of me since I had given as much as I could without expecting a reward.

The reward that I did receive was that of love. My focus was to love my mother with all I could at a time when she could not care for herself, as she had been used to doing. As I have referred earlier in this reflection, I had been self-protective of my personal boundaries since my mother was always telling me what to do or straightening my tie when I was an adult. I was not as close to her and showed her love in the way that I could. I hope that I've grown up.

The care I felt from God was awakening me to the gift of Her and her love. I felt this gift especially after my mother died and I had time to reflect on what had happened. I realized that I always looked forward to visiting her and felt comforted when I left. I understood this as knowing some of the breadth and depth of God's love from loving my mother in a way I never had.

Remembering that time leads me to reflect on what Jesus did. He did not put any limits on whom he cared for. He did not restrict when and how he gave caring to anyone, especially those in need.

To the hungry he gave food. To the homeless he shared their homelessness. To the poor he said that those with enough are expected to share with these who do not.

He included the outcast by having a meal with them and inviting them to be his followers, against the objections of the religious leaders. To the ill and maimed he gave healing. He comforted.

To those unable to find their way he gave the Spirit. To those searching for God's presence he gave words of hope and his presence of love. He gave his Father's compassion in all he did.

Jesus received care from God. Jesus relied on God for all things. He relied on God to fill his heart with compassion toward people suffering or distressed.

It is opening our hearts to God's Spirit to learn that being 'care-full' is showing compassion, kindness, goodness, reliability and all these are ways of love. This is being care-full with and for others. It is giving love from our hearts.

Who cares for us at the moment we care for others? God does. Through the Spirit He opens our hearts. God gives us people who are caregivers and gentle of heart when we need them, which is likely every day.

Being full of caring is not an obligation to satisfy God's expectations. It is not an insurance policy to guarantee our being cared for in the arms of God in heaven.

Caring is always a gift of love from God to and through us. We are called to care for particular people. The Spirit always leads us and gives us what we need to care for others, when we open our hearts to the Spirit's leading.

At the moment we care for others and give our heart and energy to them, we are opening our hearts to receive caring from God and those whom God gives us. In this way we are full of care for all others.

A Blessing
We are here to give to others. We are here to open our hearts to God and others to receive their caring.

A Prayer
Compassionate Father and Mother, lead us by your Spirit to show your caring and compassion in our daily encounters with others. Open our hearts to receive caring from you and others.

Chapter 6: Your Mind and Heart Put Right

"You're blessed when you get your inside world — your mind and heart — put right. Then you can see God in the outside world." (5:8)

We may not be aware of a need for our minds and hearts to be put right. We may not know how to recognize when our minds and hearts are not right. So, we have to ask what Jesus means by our minds and hearts being put right.

As I read the life and teachings of Jesus, I am aware that our hearts and minds are right when they are in a relationship with God that is our surrendering out will to His will. This means that God is the only one we give our lives to in daily loyalty. It is a live that desires the Spirit to transform our lives to show love, mercy, justice, integrity, gratitude, joy, friendship, and trustworthiness as Jesus did.

Our minds and hearts are not right when they are guided and have surrendered to the values and ways of society and culture. Our focus and loyalty are to being successful, prosperous, influential, social and/or politically powerful, and are esteemed by others. None of these are bad in themselves. The problem is when we make them our primary objectives and values.

These make our minds and hearts not right with God. They distract us from doing the spiritual practices that open us to God's presence and the work of the Spirit. God's way of life for us is in opposition to the ways of politics, national values, and culture.

When we commit our lives to following Christ, we are committed to being open to oneness with God, as Jesus says in his discourses in John 14-16. Loving God, others, and ourselves with our whole lives and without reserve makes our hearts and minds are the first and greatest commandment, as well as guiding us to be right with God.

Being right with God means that we open our hearts to let the Spirit guide us to have a deeper intimacy with Her. A right relationship with Her is letting the Spirit lead us to having our lives transformed through Her love and mercy. Her presence is a constant reality for our lives to which we consent.

Many Christians know about God and believe in Him. However, they have not developed a heart to heart relationship. Jesus says in Matthew 7 that telling him about all the marvelous programs and evangelizing we have done misses the boat in our relationship with God. Our hearts and minds are not right because we have not opened our hearts to God's presence and the transforming power of His love.

We discover that we cannot make our insides right by our own efforts. We do not have the strength of love and mercy that God has to transform our hearts to live right with Him and others.

The reality is that a Christian's trying to solve her or his problems without waiting for God's Spirit to guide them turns their backs on Her. They keep trying to do similar things that got them on the wrong path to begin with concerning their relationship with Her.

We may ignore the blessings of love and mercy that God gives us. We may choose not to let the Spirit lead us into a life based on the spiritual gifts of kindness, joy, love, goodness, friendship, generosity, and self-sacrifice. The consequences of this choice are not to have our minds and hearts right.

We know that the way of God's love and mercy are the right ways to live, but they are very difficult and do not provide us with the earthly treasures we crave. We may say that being right in our hearts and minds with God is an ideal but not realistic in this world.

We may eventually recognize that our hearts and minds are not right with Him. How do we make right our relationship with God and others on earth? We don't.

We admit that we are powerless to get right with God through our will power. We confess our need for God's help and especially the presence of the Spirit in our hearts. We let the Spirit lead us into acts of reconciliation with Him and with our relationships on earth. We engage in spiritual disciplines that let the Spirit fill our hearts with God's love. We live in accordance with God's love toward others.

We become right in our hearts and minds as we surrender our wills and self-centeredness to God. We follow the leading of the Spirit into a deeper relationship with Her. We become willing to know and follow Her will.

This does not mean that we will never again say or do things that cause our minds and hearts to go wrong. We are not perfect and never will be in this life. We need the Spirit to fill our hearts with be grace that God loves us warts and all. We need to remember God's love is constant and waiting our daily consent to its transforming presence in our lives.

We will go wrong at times. The amazing and wonder-filled joy is that God through the Spirit is always present to lead us back to being right.

Getting right in our minds and hearts with God enables us to see God in the larger world. We see God in the love shared with others. We see the wonders of Her creation and marvel at the connection of all parts of the universe. We see Her in the birds and plants; trees and the ocean.

We see God in acts of kindness and compassion. We see Him in acts of forgiveness and reconciliation. We see Him in the integrity of how people serve customers. We see Him in how kind and generous people are when driving. We see Him in the hungry fed, the homeless sheltered, the naked clothed, the sick cared for, the prisoner visited, and the stranger welcomed. We see Him in the spirit of cooperation and civility among politicians for the good of all the citizens.

A Blessing
We are here to open to God our hearts to receive the transforming love and mercy that leads us in the right way. We are here to look through the eyes of our hearts to see and be a part of God's love, mercy, compassion, justice, and kindness in the world.

Prayer
We desire, O Christ, to live in right relationship with you, God, and the Spirit.

Chapter 7: Cooperate Instead of Competing

"You're blessed when you can show people how to cooperate instead of compete. That's when you discover who you really are, and your place in God's family. (5:9)

This blessing seems to go against all that I was taught growing up. It certainly is in conflict with the prevailing attitude of our nation today. The common cultural wisdom is that competition is good for the buying public to receive quality at a good price.

This may have been true at one time in our nation. With the emphasis today on large salaries for executives and high dividends for investors the prevailing attitude is not competition but to grab all the money possible as quickly as possible. The advantages of competition are but a memory that is a myth advocated.

Jesus rejected competition as the way of life for Christians. This Beatitude makes it clear that the blessing from God is cooperation. Cooperation is the way to enable all participants to live together fruitfully in God's love. Cooperation is the blessing for Christians regardless of the emphasis by culture, business, and politicians on competition.

I experience this difference between cooperation and competition in a field placement in my second-year field placement in my Master's Degree Program in the School of Social Work. My project was to work with the heads of the different divisions in a regional office of the North Carolina Department of Human Resources.

My project was to work with the regional office coordinating council to develop a cooperative approach to the delivery of human services to local community agencies through the divisions of the regional office.

The regional office concept was new: different divisions of Human Resources were to cooperate to serve people in need in a defined geographical region of the state. This was almost unheard of in the 1970s since agencies had competed for recognition and funding for years.

The members of the regional office administrative council were the regional directors of the different agencies. They had little experience in a cooperation model. However, the state Human Resources Division offices were interested in this approach. They wanted to see if cooperation in the delivery of services would be more effective and less expensive. The regional offices included staff from the divisions of social service, mental health, health, vocational rehabilitation and others.

The design of my project was to develop the practical means of cooperation. The project began as expected. A couple of regional division heads were supportive of the project. The rest were skeptical but willing to give it a try. Everyone participated because their state offices required them to.

The council met weekly After about a month, we began to see the regional division directors see good possibilities with the approach. As time went on, there were some initial work in cooperation among the agencies' staff.

The process broke down after a few months at budget time. Each division had to prepare a budget for the Department of Human Resources to present to the state legislature for funding the next year. The division wanted to have as much money as possible in their budget for their staff and programs for the following year.

The budgeting and organizational systems were not set up to develop cooperative budgets for the regional offices. No one in the state office of Human Resources showed an interest in exploring a way to develop a cooperative budget that would also supported each individual division.

The state head of each division decided that cooperation was not possible with the current way of budgeting. The budgeting process ended the project. Cooperation gave way to competition, which meant that each individual regional agency had to show the best statistics they could of services their division provided, and clients served in order to increase their share of the state budget.

The training consultant in the regional office under whom I worked, and I, were disappointed. I had hoped that the cooperation model might work well enough to last into a second year. It did not. Several of the regional division heads had seen the value in this project and were disappointed that they could not continue to develop a working model.

This project is an example of the difficulty of cooperation among groups that have to compete to survive.

Another story that illustrates a need for cooperation is the 5 blind men and the elephant. As the 5 blind men walked together along a jungle road, they bumped into something they could not identify. Each laid their hands on a part of the elephant they were closest to. One said it was a wall as he laid a hand on the elephant's side. Another held the tail and said it was snake. One held a leg and said it was a massive tree. One had an ear of the elephant and said it was a plant with large leaves. One held the trunk and said it was a rope. Each insisted his description was the accurate one. They did not cooperate by sharing the information and identifying what they bumped into.

How do these experiences relate to the Beatitude above? What blessing would the regional office group have had if they could have continued to cooperate? What blessing would the 5 blind men have had if they had cooperated?

Cooperation is a skill. It has to be learned in mind and practice. It also requires that everyone involved setting aside her or his competitive ego.

The cooperative and competitive model also applies to the church. Churches try to complete with the variety of community sports and other activities that are more interesting to children and adults. Church leaders keep trying to identify what has worked to attract members and to have members again actively participate in the activities of the church. The leaders usually identified what worked when they were younger, not recognizing that they are trying to attract a different generation with different commitments and values.

Churches forget to spend time in prayer to be guided by the Spirit. They forget to ask members what they need from the church to enable them to grow in faith and services to others.

The blessing of cooperation includes the thoughts and suggestion of each person. This is how a community of faith emerges and strengthens. Cooperation is an attitude and way of life.

How, then, are we to show people how to cooperate when most people don't want to listen?

Primarily Christians are to show cooperation by how they live as Christ's community of faith being cooperative rather than competitive. Christians are to show that cooperation enables each member to contribute her or his gifts of knowledge and abilities given to them by the Spirit. This is the way that a church recognizes the leading of God in decision-making, program planning, staff hiring, and witnessing to the love and mercy of God. It trusts the Spirit of Christ to lead them to ways of cooperation.

Cooperation is a way of life that all Official Boards and committees of churches are to accept as a blessing in order to work together. Cooperation enables God's kingdom to be seen on earth as it lives for the sake of others rather than its own sake.

Members listen to the Spirit about the needs of all of the people of God and the larger community through cooperation among them, rather than using culture experiences of competition. The Spirit will lead them to ask how are they inclusive, respectful, and loving toward each other and the larger community?

This is how we know who we are. We are the people of God who live the way and the truth of God's love and mercy. We live the way of forgiveness and reconciliation. We live the way of generosity, kindness, and oneness as the body of Christ. We live the way of trusting and relying on God by waiting for Her guidance. We especially live this way with the poor, powerless, vulnerable, homeless, and others considered unworthy of our attention. We live God's cooperation, instead of culture's competition.

The life of cooperation is not easy. Most church members find it is easier to follow the way of competition that is more familiar from everyday work groups and volunteer organizations. We need the Spirit to lead us to live God's will for the least as well as the influential. The way of cooperation takes time and perseverance so that our hearts become one in Her to make cooperation a way of life.

A Blessing
We are here to live together as brothers and sisters in Christ to live by the leading of the Spirit to cooperative rather than compete.

A Prayer
Spirit of peace and cooperation, I desire your presence to enable me to live and witness to the live of cooperation that comes from your love.

Chapter 8: Persecution

"You are blessed when your commitment to God provokes persecution. The persecution drives you even deeper into God's kingdom." (5:10)

Jesus did not say that we are persecuted for what we believe. He said that his followers would be persecuted for taking seriously his teachings of living the ways of God's kingdom that expects those with power to take care of the powerless.

Jesus refers in this Beatitude to persecution of his followers based on their commitment to following God's way of life as Jesus was. They live according to the values and ways of God than of the cultural values and the nation's way of justice and love.

In Luke 4 Jesus delivers a sermon in Nazareth on the nature of God's kingdom and the Christian life. The people listened. They became upset with him with he referred to ministering to other nations and cultures. They wanted Jesus to make his permanent home in Nazareth that they would have the distinction of being the home and resident of this teacher and healer. This would give them status that other cities and towns in Galilee did not have. When Jesus refused to be whom the people of Nazareth wanted and was ready to leave the town, the people were so angry that they led him to a cliff to throw him off.

He refused to live the way they expected. They were ready to persecute him by killing him. It did not happen. He knew that God was present with him and would determine when the time of Jesus' death suited Her time and plan.

The point was that Jesus chose to live the way of God's kingdom. His way of life was usually at odds with Jewish religious traditions, yet, reflected the intentions God had in His laws and the purpose of Israel for which he saved them from slavery. He usually associated those whom the religious leaders identified as outcasts and sinners by eating with them, spending time with them, and making them his disciples.

Jesus says at the Last Supper recorded in John 15:18-20a: **"If you find the godless world is hating you, remember it got its start hating me. If you lived on the world's terms, the world would love you as one of its own. But since I picked you to live on God's terms and no longer on the world's terms, the world is going to hate you. When that happens, remember this: Servants don't get better treatment than their masters..."**

Jesus says that we experience persecution as he did, when we live according to the ways of God's love and mercy. The Christian way of life is based on how we live daily the way of God's kingdom. Too often persecutions come from Christians toward other Christians.

Jesus says that persecution comes when we choose to live in opposition to the ways of culture that we have heard inside and outside the church for years. We are to live the Christian life as Jesus' teaches in the Sermon on the Mount. This will lead us to living according to God's kingdom, rather that according the expectations and teachings of the culture or society. It will lead us to a life of love, mercy, justice, peace, joy, and gratitude.

Persecution comes when we live the Beatitudes and the spiritual gifts of God. It comes because of our way of life rather than the dogmas or moralisms we believe.

A Blessing

We are here to let the Spirit lead us to live the way of love and mercy in our daily lives and not just as a private experience kept within our souls. We are here to accept the negative reactions of others toward us because we commit our lives to God's life and not the life of the world or culture.

A Prayer

Merciful God, I desire the courage to live your kingdom way according to the teachings of Jesus and the leading of your Spirit.

Chapter 9: In Good Company

"Not only that — count yourself blessed every time people put you down or throw you out or speak lies about you to discredit me. What it means is that the truth is too close for comfort and they are uncomfortable. You can be glad when that happens — give a cheer, even! — for though you don't like it, *I* do! And all heaven applauds. And know that you are in good company. My prophets and witnesses have always gotten into this kind of trouble." (5:11-12)

I have known a few men and women who spoke God's words from scripture that made people uncomfortable. I read about men and women in the 1970s that acted in protest against war and nuclear weapons. Many were jailed.

I read about preachers who made church members uncomfortable enough with sermons against the wars in Vietnam and Iraq. These preachers were often forced to leave as pastor of churches. Other churches and pastors talked and prayed whether they could be the church with differences of social and political beliefs.

Christians make people uncomfortable when they quote Jesus about such things as loving enemies, helping the poor move from survival to thriving, and building a homeless shelter in a residential neighborhood or business section of town. Other church members gossip about other Christians who live the truth way of Christ rather than the false way of society and culture. The gossip does not have to be completely true.

Jesus says to his disciples at the Last Supper recorded in John 15:21-25: **"They (the people of the world) are going to do all these things to you because of the way they treated me, because they don't know the one who sent me. If I hadn't come and told them all this in plain language, it wouldn't be so bad. As it is, they have no excuse. Hate me, Hate my Father—it's all the same. If I hadn't done what I have done among them, works no one has *ever* done, they wouldn't be to blame. But they saw the God-signs and hated anyway, both my Father and me. Interesting—they have verified the truth of their own Scriptures where it is written, 'They hated me for no good reason.'"**

Followers of Jesus belong to a body of believers who are to have and share a faith journey that follows Jesus the Christ daily. They consent to the Spirit transform their hearts to live a new life in Christ. They are persecuted because they are committed to the new life given in and through Christ. They are persecuted because they follow the way, truth, and life of God revealed in Christ.

Persecution is not limited to imprisonment or torture. Persecution occurs through gossip and falsely accusing. It occurs when followers of Jesus are lied about or left out of activities that they use to be invited to participate in. I talked of this more fully in the last reflection.

Notice that Jesus says that we are being persecuted to *discredit him* (italics added). Why would anyone seek to discredit Jesus? How do people discredit us in order to discredit Jesus?

People today may discredit Jesus by saying his life and teachings are ideals. They do not believe the ideals could be lived in our daily lives.

Scripture gives us a different perspective about living the Christian life. The prophets of Israel, Jesus, and Paul assumes that God's way of life is the real way. The ways of the world are not real since they are created by us and not by God.

Many church members don't want to hear that we are to produce fruits of faith through the Spirit of Christ. Jesus taught this. Paul listed the fruits in Galatians 5:22-23. We are to produce fruits of the Spirit as the beautiful apple and orange blossoms become fruit. Our faith is to also produce fruits.

Jesus said that we are the branches connected to him, our vine. As branches we are to produce fruits. In the Sermon on the Mount Jesus warns about false preachers who talk a lot but do not produce the fruits of faith. God expects us to produce fruits that include willingness to be faithful to our commitment to Her; to be alive with a sense of compassion for people who are different; and a conviction that God's holiness permeates things and people.

We cannot live Christ's way by following rigidly a legal set of laws. Memorizing laws is unlikely to create a heart to heart relationship with God. It is unlikely to produce fruits of the kingdom of Him.

Among those who belong to Christ, everything connected with their egocentricity was crucified. The Spirit awakens us to rely on the presence and love of God rather than our self-centered egos.

Jesus calls us to a different way of life based on our relationships with God. Among this different way of life is that we are called to be ministers of reconciliation in our daily lives. (See II Corinthians 5:16-20)

It is unpleasant being lied about and put down because we consent to the Spirit's transforming our hearts to live as Christ lived on earth. We don't want to be cast out from our friends, family, or Social or political groups for speaking the truth that we have received from Jesus through the work of the Spirit. We don't want to be ignored by others because our way of life in Christ is different from the more accepted ways of culture.

Given the suffering we may face and the discomfort we may receive from those around us why would Jesus and all in heaven applaud our being lied about, ignored, be gossiped about, and being physically threatened?

Jesus' joy is that our persecution occurs because we are living by word and deed the truth of God's love and mercy. We are witnessing to the life founded on love that He gives us, and we can see manifested in him. We are caring for the poor, powerless, stranger, and outcast.

We are neither the first nor the last that will be put down, thrown out, and lied about for witnessing to the truth of Jesus to love one another as God loves us. The Sermon is about living a heart to heart relationship with Her in our daily lives. It is about living the way and truth of Christ as a community of brothers and sisters in Christ.

We have Christ, the Spirit, and the church community present to help us keep our hearts open to Christ and one another.

A Blessing

We are here to live the truth of God's love and mercy. We are here to rejoice with Christ and all of heaven when the truth of God is proclaimed in our daily lives.

A Prayer

Christ of new life, I desire the courage to live this new life of love you give me, even when it leads to being lied about, put down, or made an outcast.

Chapter 10: The God-flavor Salt

"Let me tell you why you are here. You're here to be salt seasoning that brings out the God-flavors of the earth. If you lose your saltiness, how will people taste godliness? You've lost your usefulness and will end up in the garbage." (5:13)

Very rarely have I preachers and seminar leaders ask their listeners what the listeners consider the purpose of the Christian life. They seem more to ask the question of purpose as are the people saved and believe they are going to heaven.

A few years ago, a bestselling book focused on the Christian life in terms of it being a purpose driven life. The focus seemed to be that a Christian was to find out what God wanted them to do and let that purpose drive their live in all that they do.

Some people say that God has a purpose for everyone. They believe that what happens in a Christian's life always has a purpose from God. We may not know at the time what purpose an event has in the life of a Christian. But, some people are convinced that God has a purpose for whatever happens.

We just finished reflecting on the Beatitudes. The Beatitudes turn out to be a series of blessings that God gives Christian. The blessings are to be lived by Christians in the world. The Beatitudes are what is to drive the life of a Christian.

Throughout the Sermon Jesus presents the Christian life on earth as different from the success oriented and self-centered life promoted by our culture and affirmed by our little egos.

Jesus tells us in these three verses what we are to do to live the Beatitudes and the rest of the teachings of the Sermon. These verses tell us how to live the true self that God gives us. They define the true purpose of the Christian life.

The big emphasis in the church of my teenage years was soul winning, as I mentioned above. The leaders of our teenage group showed us how to win souls using the 'Roman Road to Salvation." We listened to the leader and underlined the passages in Romans that would lead others to salvation,

I never used it. I did not feel comfortable talking to people about the Roman Road to salvation. All the people I knew were saved and members of churches. If there were unsaved people, I did not know them. I was also too uncomfortable approaching others to talk about the Roman Road to salvation.

Later in my life I looked again at this Roman Road. I saw that the passages seemed to have been selected to put the fear of punishment into people. The verses were full of judgment and condemnation of people. The emphasis was that those who did not walk the Roman Road of salvation would be punished.

By this time the Spirit was leading me to know about God's saving love and clearing my heart of the threats of Hell and its fire that I had first learned.

The Roman Road to salvation is not God's way of giving us our new life in Christ. This way is not God's way of transforming love.

God gives Her love to us without feeling that we are terrible sinners. She did not create the Roman Road of salvation. It really goes against the primary emphasis in scripture of God's love and mercy. She gives us the Spirit that we may enter into Her love and come to love Her heart to heart.

Jesus takes a different approach to describing the purpose of the Christian life. He divides the living of the Christian life into two ways. They are not ways of belief. They are the ways of our consenting to have God present in our lives and the Spirit guiding our lives. Jesus says that the purpose of the Christian life is to be God-flavoring and God-coloring in the world.

What does a Christian live God-flavoring in the world?

Most translation uses the image of salt. Salt is a seasoning that brings out flavors in food. In our relationship with God, the salt seasoning of faith brings out the God-flavors of love, mercy, joy, kindness, goodness, faithfulness, peace, friendship, justice, and humility. All of these ways of relating are expressions of God's love.

We give salt seasoning as Jesus did. He loved all he met. We are to do the same as followers of Christ. He healed. We work toward everyone having good medical care, as well as praying for them to be healed. He accepts the reality of human imperfection. We accept the imperfections of others and us. He includes outsiders by inviting the poor and outcasts to a banquet He is giving. This is not easy for most of us as it was in Jesus' day.

St. Paul describes the salt-flavors in Galatians 5:13-21:

"My counsel is this: Live free, animated and motivated by God's Spirit. Then you won't feed the compulsions of selfishness. For there is a root of sinful self-interest in us that is at odds with a free spirit, just as the free spirit is incompatible with selfishness.

These two ways of life are antithetical, so that we cannot live at times one way and at times another way according to how we feel on any given day. Why don't we choose to be led by the Spirit and so escape the erratic compulsions of a law-dominated existence?

It is obvious what kind of life develops out of trying to get your own way all the time: repetitive, loveless, cheap sex, a stinking accumulation of mental and emotional garbage; frenzied and joyless grabs for happiness; trinket gods; magic-show religion; paranoid loneliness; cutthroat competition; all-consuming-yet-never satisfied wants; a brutal temper; and importance to love or be loved; divided homes and divided lives small-minded and lopsided pursuits; the vicious habit of depersonalizing everyone into a rival; uncontrolled and uncontrollable additions; ugly parodies of communities."

What happens when we live God's salt-flavoring way? He gives us gifts to share, which are the fruits of our lives as Christians. The fruits come on the branches of our lives that are attached to the vine of Christ. The fruits include affection and compassion for others. It is exuberance about life, serenity, control, faithfulness, friendship, and goodness.

We develop a willingness to stick with thing, a sense of compassion in our hearts, and a conviction that God is present in all things and people making them holy. We find ourselves involved in loyal commitments that enable to marshal and direct our energies wisely.

Since this is a new kind of life we are given, let us make sure that we do not just hold it as an idea in our heads or a sentiment in our hearts. God's love is present to transform our hearts and mind to giving God's love to others and to recognize God's presence in all things and people.

That means we will not compare ourselves with each other as if one of us were right and going to Heaven, while another was wrong and going to Hell. We have far more important things to do without lives, such as feed the hungry, cloth the naked, give shelter to the homeless. We are to let the Spirit join our hearts with God's that we may know His love and share that love with others.

Our purpose is to be God's love on earth daily. We are not to pretend loving others. We are not to be an expert on God's love, quoting scripture to describe it. We are to open our hearts to the Spirit to make us the loving God-flavor with whom we are with and where we are.

A Blessing

We are here for the purpose to daily add salt seasoning to the earth to bring out the God-flavors in the lives of all persons and of the universe.

A Prayer

Loving God, by your Spirit transform my life into salt seasoning love that flavors my relationships on earth with your love and mercy.

Chapter 11: The Light of God-colors

"Here's another way to put it: You're here to be light, bringing out the God-colors in the world. God is not a secret to be kept. We're going public with this, as public as a city on a hill. If I make you light-bearers, you don't think I'm going to hide you under a bucket, do you? I'm putting you on a light stand. Now that I've put you there on a hilltop, on a light stand—shine! Keep open house; be generous with your lives. By opening up to others, you'll prompt people to open up with God, this generous Father in heaven." (5:14-16)

God's light has many colors. It has colors for healing, giving hope to the poor, taking the side of the powerless, and letting God's laws take president over human interpretation and establishing a tradition based on this. It has light that invites you and gives you the Spirit to fill your life with God's love and transforming presence as you desire and welcome it throughout your life. God's light comes through Christ to enable us to open our hearts to the Spirit who leads us to share our light from God with the world.

We see the universe with our eyes with the help of the stars and the reflections of moons and planets. We can see the vastness of the universe with the powerful telescopes on earth and in space.

Darkness also pervades the universe and our lives. The universe looks dark without the stars. Darkness also pervades our lives that are dominated by our self-centeredness. Without the indwelling of Christ in our hearts, we have no light of God to share with the world.

John 1 says that darkness cannot overcome the light of God. God's light gives color to the world. God gave the rainbow to Noah as His promise of giving Her light in the world. She gave the rainbow as the sign of always being faithful to Her promise. How does the color of God's light shine in the universe?

God shines colors through us. They are the colors of our living the light of love and mercy that He gives us. It is the color of redemption and reconciliation. It is the color of new life that overcomes the living deaths of self-centeredness or neglect by those who could support a decent living for those without.

Other living deaths include the death of relationships from the darkness of personal selfishness. It is the death of lies. It is the death of being critical and judgmental of others because they are not like us or think as we do. It is the death from being isolated. Our world seems to thrive on the darkness of self-destruction, chaos, war, greed, and self-centeredness.

God gives the light of love, mercy, inclusion, justice, and compassion through Christ. God's gift of a different way of life from culture leads us to live the love that often means we are ignored or rejected as Christ was.

God makes us Her light bearers in the world. She sits us on a hill that God's light may be seen through us from miles away. She makes us lamps that give light to a dark house. She shines light through us to the life of people we meet daily.

How do we become light-bearers? We consent to letting God's love shine through us. We let the Spirit give us the courage to shine God's light knowing we may be ridiculed or rejected. We also feel great joy in being God's light whether rejected or accepted.

There are also ways in which we hide our light from God. We put shades on our light. We are reluctant to be God's light since it shines on the sins and selfish in our world including our own. We don't let the Spirit change our lives to be God's light, since the culture's way of lighting one's way is so much more enticing and self-fulfilling.

God's light redeems the universe. It is the energy that creates and holds together all things. It cannot be overwhelmed by the darkness that surrounds it. He reveals His light in Christ who was present at Creation and throughout eternity.

We are not flashlights that God turns on and off. We are Her constant light shining in and through us. She uses us as light bearers not because we are perfect lights, but because She is.

God shines enough light through us to illuminate the places we journey daily. He enables our light to extent to the universe to which we are connected through His love. He gives us His light gratuitously and we consent to be as generous with His light to others.

A Blessing
We are here to be filled with God's light and to let the Spirit shine Her light through us.

A Prayer
Light of the world, you enable me to be the light of your love on earth that transform your creation into your colors.

Chapter 12: Jesus Completes the Law

"Don't suppose for a minute that I have come to demolish the Scriptures—either God's Law or the Prophets. I'm not here to demolish but to complete. I am going to put it all together, pull it all together in a vast panorama. God's Law is more real and lasting than the stars in the sky and the ground at your feet. Long after stars burn out and earth wears out, God's Law will be alive and working." (5:17-18)

As I was growing up in church, God's Laws referred primarily to the Ten Commandments. There were other writings in the Old Testament that church leaders said we must also obey. They were usually moralistic laws. They were used to judge people's Christian living and whether they were faithful Christians.

When I think about it, I do not remember much being said about the Prophets. I do not remember sermons or study lessons that focused on the law that Jesus said is the first commandment: love God and love neighbor, as we love ourselves.

The Prophets speak for God about how we are to *live* the Law. The Prophets primarily focused on the ways the religious leaders and the wealthy mistreated the poor and powerless by not assuring the latter had enough to let them thrive. The religious leaders and wealthy were so involved in increasing their power and wealth that they spent little time beyond the prescribed letter of the laws that they did not consider the desires of God toward taking care of the vulnerable, powerless, and poor. According to the Prophets, God's law is about relationships built on God's love. The Law is a living and dynamic code.

The laws are about God's way of life that He created for us to make visible with the help of the Spirit. They are our part in God's revealing His kingdom on earth as it is in heaven. The Prophets spoke to Israel in the name of God on their need to repeat and live life according to God's loving laws rather than wealth and power. They were faithful to the letter of the Law because most wanted to impress God and receive material blessings from God and esteem from other humans.

Jesus fulfilled the words of the Prophets with his healing and setting people free from sin. He summarized this in his only sermon in Nazareth by reading Isaiah 61:1-2: "The Spirit of God, the Master, is on me because God anointed me. He sent me to preach good news to the poor, heal the heartbroken, announce freedom to all captives, and pardon all prisoners. God sent me to announce the year of his grace — a celebration of God's destruction of our enemies — and to comfort all who mourn."

Jesus said that he has not come to do away with the Law or Prophets. He has come to fulfill them. I need to be clear what I understand Jesus is referring to.

Is Jesus saying that he is affirming the Laws and Prophets as I heard proclaimed in church? Am I supposed to take the laws literally and follow them word for word?

Is he saying that we are to follow all of the Law? Where do the Prophets fit in?

Jesus says that he has come to fulfill what God intended for Israel through the laws. The Spirit leads me to understand this verse as pertaining to the relationship between God and us. He is not giving Israel the Commandments as a law book that He took an evening to write and give to Moses. He is giving Israel and us a way of life.

This verse refers to the relationship that the laws were intended to for us to have with God and all others. God's Law is not a book filled with laws to be memorized and recited to prove that we know the laws of God. The Scribes and Pharisees had understood the Laws as requirements to follow literally in order to live a righteous life. They interpreted the laws as what God requires of us to be in right relationship with Him. Jesus says that he has come to fulfill the intent God has in giving the laws.

In this passage and the next one, Jesus shows us the intent of the Law. He tells us how the Law is about relationships that mature as we grow in faith. They are not intended as a list of things to obey. We understand this better as we look closely at the Ten Commandments to see that they speak of relating to God and to neighbor in love.

A Blessing
We are here to let the Spirit lead us to live in our daily lives the law of love that we receive from God.

A Prayer
God of love and mercy, I desire your Spirit to clean out the corrupted law in my heart and mind and to fill me with the intent of your laws.

Chapter 13: Don't Trivialize the Law

"Trivialize even the smallest item in God's Law and you will only have trivialized yourself. But take it seriously, show the way for others, and you will find honor in the kingdom. Unless you do far better than the Pharisees in the matters of right living, you won't know the first thing about entering the kingdom." (5:19-20)

This passage baffled me initially. I grew with Christians who interpreted the laws of God to their benefit. One was 'children obey your parent' without also including 'parents do not provoke your children.' Another was for wives to obey their husbands without also including that husbands should love their wives. Another was that the poor we always have with us as an excuse to not take care of them. God's laws are all about relating in love and unity with God and in love with each other.

How do we trivialize ourselves? By using it to obey our wants at the expense of other and of our relationship with God. Any time we make a law serve our views or actions is to trivialize ourselves.

The churches I attended taught me that God's Law is to be strictly obeyed. They made obeying the Law more important than grace, even though they talked a lot about grace. They made salvation contingent upon obeying the Law.

I heard then and still hear among many Christians today that it is necessity to obey God's Law in order for us to be acceptable to Her and to be saved. They use 'obeying' to mean knowing the laws and doing exactly what the Law says.

Many teachers and preachers say that Christians are to memorize the Law, especially the Ten Commandments, and follow them to the letter. This view of the Law may be one significant way in which we trivialize the Law.

We do not use the law for loving God and our neighbor. We use the Law to justify our actions and impress God and others.

Contrary to the thinking and words of many Christians, obeying the Law literally is not avoiding punishment in hell (which is separation from God by making the Law more important than love of God and neighbor). The Law in its intent is about living in relationship of love with God and one another.

I began to think of the ways that we might trivialize the Law without noticing that we are doing it. We may trivialize the Law by believing its only purpose is to save us from hell. Another way of trivializing the Law is selecting verses to support our social, religious, or political point of view, even when that is not the intent of the verses.

The Law and the Prophets are about the way we live our faith. They speak God's word to us that we may know the ways She loves.

Paul said in Romans 7:7-8 that without clear guidelines from the Law for right moral behavior would be mostly guess work. He gives the example of the Law making him aware of 'coveting.'

Paul says without the Law he would not know that coveting the property of others is not an act of God's love. He says that the Law on coveting is about our loving relationship with our neighbors and not a legal requirement that we fulfill to please God.

If I use the Laws as the means for tying my hands so that I will not steal someone else's possession, then I assume being in charge of preventing my covenanting the possessions of others. I am not relying on God to lead me in love to refrain from theft.

I follow the leading of sin to live by my personal desires rather than God's love. I am also making God's Law unimportant except to prevent me from stealing, killing, adultery, or lying. I am not letting the Spirit lead me through prayer and scripture to engage in a loving relationship with God and with others.

Treating the Law as not about loving relationship is opposed to relying on the Law to give life totally to God's love. I trivialize myself by requiring some form of restraint other than God's love to keep control of my behaviors and my relationships with other people. I may need this early in my faith. I am to mature in faith to live God's loving relationship with God and others.

A Blessing
We are here to learn from God's Law how our lives are different from the ways of the world.

A Prayer
God, Christ, Spirit, bring me into your community that I may live based on the gift of your Law that opens my eyes to your presence and loving you.

Chapter 14: Anger and Murder

"You're familiar with the command to the ancients, 'Do not murder.' I'm telling you that anyone who is so much as angry with a brother or sister is guilty of murder." (5:21-22)

This is the first of 6 antitheses in which Jesus contrasts the interpretation of a law of God by the Pharisees and the intent of God's law. His understanding comes from God since he is one with God. Jesus seems to use exaggeration in reveal the intent of the law to his hearers.

We may think that Jesus is unrealistic to claim that being angry with someone is the same as murder. Taken literally Jesus' statement would mean that any time we are angry at someone it is the same as murdering them. There is no denying that we may feel like 'strangling' someone who makes us very angry. Most of us do not act on the threatening words we use toward another when we are angry.

Why, then, would Jesus say that being angry with someone would be the same as killing him or her? Why would he take angry words to be the same as murder when we do not intend any physical harm to the person that we are angry at?

Some people may do physical harm or even murder when they are angry at someone. We have read stories of women stabbing or shooting a spouse or office co-workers because they are angry to the point of being enraged and feel the need to act and to release the rage.

We know that Jesus does not made statements without trying to convey a deeper truth to his listeners. He does not call attention to himself with such exaggerations. Therefore, we need to seek the meaning he is giving us behind his words.

First, we consider what God is showing us in Her laws. We know that murder is not acceptable to Her. Even some soldiers who are Christians wrestle with their conscious when facing an enemy whom they must kill or who will kill them.

Some people salve their conscious with the Old Testament passages that say that God told Israel to go to war and to destroy their enemies. They also quote the text out of context of an eye for an eye. These verses, however, do not agree with God's command to love our enemies, as we love our friends and family.

Discussing Jesus' teaching in this passage is more complex than it appears. What we need to remember is that God is a God of love and mercy. The Ten Commandments were given as a way for Israel to life each day in relationship with God and others. They are not just a set of laws to obey. The Ten Commandments describe how we live in loving relationship with God: worshiping no other gods and spending the Sabbath renewing our bodies and souls. The Commandments described how we are to love other people: not lying, not stealing, not lusting, and not killing.

God gave Israel the Ten Commandments that Israel would create a nation different from other nations. He desired that Israel would base its life on love and compassion for one another. It was not to base its life on the grab for power, success, security, and esteem by the king, the priest, and the wealthy. That is what other nations do. It is not how God loves and has mercy on all people. It is how Israel was to show all nations what it means to live daily in and through God's love. I

In this way Israel would be the light of God's love, mercy, and justice to all nations. Israel would live the way God intends all nations and persons to live together. Its life would bring all nations to God's mountain to learn of Him and the Torah, as Isaiah 2 says.

God created the world for people to live with one another in peace and love, justice, mercy, kindness, and compassion. The scriptures describe how humans chose to pursue their ego desires, including killing to obtain what they want, rather than pursuing God's intention of love and mercy that comes from Her. The scriptures speak to choosing a life opposite form self-centeredness.

The issue is about more than killing. Not killing is restraining ourselves with rules and regulations. God wants our relationships to be more than using our will power to restrict our destructive way of life. The issue is relating with others with the same love and mercy with which God related to the people of Israel and continues to relate with us.

Anger becomes the same as murder when we stop loving others. We depersonalize people and stop relating to them. We kill relationships with self-centeredness and egocentric demands. People die to us in our heart and mind. We end up avoiding them and ignoring them.

God calls us to be His people of reconciliation and forgiveness. He blesses us with a humble heart and mind that seeks cooperation rather than competition. He leads us to live so that when hostility may arise in us His love is strong and deep enough to transform our anger and behaviors.

It is not easy to live so that hostility does not dominate our feelings and behaviors. It is not easy to find a way to defend ourselves from the anger of another that seeks to enable them not to sin by murder and to seek the love of God already in them by which they relate with all people.

What can we do to heal the anger that fills our hearts? What can we do to let the Spirit lead us to give our anger to God and to forgive whom we are angry at?

It takes a desire for the indwelling of the Spirit. The Spirit can lead us as we are ready to let go of our anger to a different way of life. The Spirit can do this as we open our hearts to God's presence and love and as the Spirit transforms our hearts to live more fully God's love.

We seek discernment of God's way from the Spirit. It takes courage to admit our anger and open our hearts to the Spirit to transform our lives to the way of love.

In the end we seek to keep alive the relationships that God has given us. We choose not to be the one to kill the relationships or physically kill people. We let the Spirit lead us to another way of life that shows the truth of God's love and mercy.

A Blessing
We are here to let the Spirit lead us to live in forgiving relationships with others.

A Prayer
My desire, O Christ, is for your Spirit to lead me to live more consistently your love and mercy.

Chapter 15: Make Things Right with Brothers and Sisters in Christ

"This is how I want you to conduct yourself in these matters. If you enter your place of worship and, about to make an offering, you suddenly remember a grudge a friend has against you, abandon your offering, leave immediately, go to this friend and make things right. Then and only then, come back and work things out with God." (5:23-24)

Reflecting on these two verses I understand more clearly the connection between God and us and the relationship between brothers and sisters in Christ. I was especially struck by the emphasis Jesus places on our worship with our broken relationship with our brothers and sisters in Christ. I followed most people and did not think about the need to be reconciled with others before worshipping God.

I grew up believing that worship is more of an individual experience with God done in a place with other Christians. Worship leaders did not invite us to be reconciled with one another and to be joined in heart and mind with other worshippers through passing the peace. What people thought about each other did not occur to me as important to our worship of God.

Churches do not seem to give as much emphasis on forgiveness and reconciliation in a worship service among members as to preaching and music to praise God. The majority of members have a good relationship with one another, as evident by all the talking done before the organ prelude.

Those who do not get along ignore one another and sit on opposite sides of the sanctuary. If the rift is bad enough, one or both individuals and families do not attend worship at all, except on special occasions.

Why are love and mercy with fellow members important before worshipping God? Reconciliation within churches witnesses to the centrality of reconciliation with God. It is important to the reconciliation within the kingdom of God by being reconciled with our brothers and sisters in Christ regardless to what church they belong.

Every Sunday most churches include the Lord's Prayer in their worship. We ask God to forgive us as we forgive others. This states a direct relationship between our relationship with brothers and sisters in Christ and our worship of God.

Asking forgiveness of another person is necessary to reconciliation. It acknowledges that we know that we have hurt the heart of a fellow Christian. However, asking forgiveness is not easy.

We have to admit that we have hurt a brother or sister in Christ, whether intentionally or not. We acknowledge that we have caused harm by our selfish actions or words.

We may ask what makes reconciling with another important, especially before we enter into worship? Worship focuses on our relationship with God. God has already forgiven us. We come to Him individually or in corporate worship to deepen our relationship and admit that we have acted or spoken in ways that hurt others and cause a rift between us. This includes making our confession, asking forgiveness, and accepting His forgiveness that is already present in our hearts through the Spirit.

Let us remember that the most important commandment is to love God and our neighbors as ourselves. Worship is not simply about singing hymns, reading scripture, saying prayers, or preaching. It is about the deepening of our relationship with God that makes us one with and in Her through deepening our oneness in heart with one another.

We are one with Her through Christ. We are one with brothers and sisters in Christ because we join together in living the way of love and mercy.

Worship draws us together. We cannot be drawn together when we are separated from God and one another because we have refrained from engaging in forgiveness and reconciliation

We open our hearts for God to cleanse them of our little egos that lead us to be self-centered and judgmental. The Spirit is able then to fill our hearts with God's love and mercy with our desire and consent. We consent to God's presence in our lives--our hearts and minds--that we may be transformed to a life based on love and mercy. Then we are humbled enough to ask of other forgiveness, receive forgiveness, and engage in reconciliation.

A Blessing
We are here to worship God when we are reconciled with brothers and sisters in Christ, which opens us to be reconciled with Her

A Prayer
Spirit of God, I need your guidance and courage to risk admitting when I hurt my brothers and sisters in Christ and to seek reconciliation.

Chapter 16: Make Things Right with an Enemy

"Or say you're out on the street and an old enemy accosts you. Don't lose a minute. Make the first move; make things right with him. After all, if you leave the first move to him, knowing his track record, you're likely to end up in court, maybe even jail. If that happens, you won't get out without a stiff fine." (5:25-26)

My first reaction to this verse is I don't want to be in jail. There are many things that I read about jails and prisons that I don't want to experience: the confinement, the rigid life, the toughs, and the hostile attitude of prison personnel and other prisoners. When men and women have served their prison time, they are often isolated by society. They often have a difficult time obtaining work to support themselves, much less a family. They are ostracized. They often do not trust others and are angry at who treats them with contempt and shows them a lack of respect.

The last line of the passage, needless to say, got my attention. I could imagine doing almost anything to persuade an enemy not to go to court.

After some reflection, I realized that Jesus was likely not using 'prison' as a scare tactic. He was not using 'jail' to motivate us to engage in reconciliation that he was teaching regarding our enemies.

If Christians find it difficult to reconcile with brothers and sisters in Christ, we probably find it more difficult reconciling with enemies. I assume that the enemy Jesus is describing is one with a grudge against us that he or she wants to avenge.

Enemies are not likely to hold the same values the followers of Jesus do about forgiveness and reconciliation. They do not live by God's love and mercy.

Jesus' also implies that we are likely to lose a court case. He does not say why. My thought is that the law does not favor the poor whom was the focus of Jesus' ministry.

So, what are we to do? How are we to approach the enemy with a hope of settling the problem out of court?

We are to pray to God seeking the help of the Spirit. We are to trust God to be present and to do what is right for us according to His will. We are to use our most humble, compassionate, kind, and loving selves to relate with an enemy.

We have no control over the decision of the enemy. We may go to court. Only God and the heart of our enemy can decide to accept our offer of reconciliation. If we are sentenced to jail, we are to continue to rely on God, since She will be present with us through the scare and turmoil to comfort us, to be attached with us in love, and to hear our prayers.

The point is that we approach our enemy with love and mercy. We admit our wrong. We confess our part in the problem. We ask for forgiveness. We offer to make amends for the wrong we have done the enemy.

We seek to reconcile with the enemy that we may continue to serve God in our daily lives and travels outside of prison. If we go to jail, we continue to serve God as directed by the Spirit.

If we go to jail, God may give us other Christians with whom to worship and share our faith. It is likely that we shall also experience persecution in prison for living our faith.

Jesus says later in the Sermon that we are to love our enemies and do good to those who despitefully use us. We'll need to remember this passage when we confront our enemies.

All that I have said may sound idealistic to many people. Others may say that what I say sounds good, but it will not work in the real world. They would say the best advice is to get a better lawyer.

Yet, what I have described is what is real for God. She has given Her Law, the words of the Prophets, and the incarnation of Christ to show us that Her reality is our illusion. We may not have had enough people living this way to guide us in reconciling with our enemies regardless of what it may cost emotionally, spiritually, physically, or materially.

A Blessing
We are here to live the kingdom of God's love by seeking reconciliation with our enemies.

A Prayer
Spirit of Christ, it is not easy for me to face an enemy. I need your help.

Chapter 17: Lust Corrupts Hearts

"You know the next commandment pretty well, too: 'Don't go to bed with another's spouse." But don't think you've preserved your virtue simply by staying out of bed. Your *heart* can be corrupted by lust even quicker than your *body*. Those leering looks you think nobody notices—they also corrupt." (5:27-28)

In the passage above Jesus refers to a person's virtue being affected by adultery. The Greek word for virtue usually refers to our hearts, or more specifically the core of our beings. This understanding of virtue is in keeping with a central theme of Jesus' teachings.

Jesus refers to the heart throughout the Sermon as the core of our lives. Here as elsewhere Jesus is referring to the meaning and depth of relationships at the time between men and women. Today he would also refer to all relationships regardless of gender or sexual orientation. Adultery is experienced in all these relationships by what one partner of a couple does and how it affects her/his heart.

Some relationships outside of marriage are only physical. Some look for the emotional and physical intimacy not found in the marriage. Some persons are falling in love and growing in the depth of intimacy, often because this kind of love felt absent from the relationship by one or both spouses. It may be also that the couple does not adjust their relationship to the needs of the other or the changes that come with years of marriage or committed relationship.

Jesus, I assume, is describing what a difference the real presence of God's love makes in a marriage. He is saying that marriages are different when the two bring to it a deepening faith in Her love and a desire to live and grow in the marriage within the context of this love.

God is concerned not simply with how well the couple follows the civil and biblical laws regarding marriage. He is concerned with our letting the Spirit lead us separately into Christ's way of life, and to lead the marriage into being a two-person version of the body of Christ. How else can we say with honesty that the two have been joined together by Him unless both desire the Spirit to lead them to become one, as we desire the Spirit to lead us into being one heart with God?

The virtue that Jesus refers to is not simply one quality of life among many. It is our daily, committed way of life. It is not only obeying the rules for a faithful life with God. It is having our lives transformed to live constantly a virtuous life. It is opening the center of our beings, our hearts, for the Spirit to lead us into receiving a new life.

Marriage is not easy. Children, jobs, and other responsibilities are added to the couple to include in growing in the marriage itself. The two may not spend as much time together. They may forget to do the small loving things for each other that keep the marriage alive. Many feel an emptiness but do not talk about it.

There grows a deepening desire in a person's heart to have what they feel missing in their marriage or committed relationship. They may find a particular person whom they lust for in the hope they the new person can give them what they desire.

Jesus says that lust in the heart is just the same as physical intimacy. Lust is adultery because it seeks gratification in a relationship that only has its rightful place in marriage or a committed relationship. Adultery degrades the virtue in the center of our souls.

Each partner in a marital relationship has other relationships. This is not a criticism of the marriage. This is the recognition that a person needs a variety of relationships with friends who can meet needs that are not met by the partners in a marriage. However, there are limitations that each partner honors that would adversely affect their partner and commitment.

To live virtuous lives in and through God requires letting go of having our little egos run our lives seeking selfish pleasure. A virtuous life requires that we desire to let the Spirit cleanse our hearts of our egocentricity and to fill them with God's love and mercy.

Our choosing against adultery relationships is based on and an expression of God's love. The choice to honor the partner and their commitment enhances the virtue at the core of our being. The choice against adultery comes out of the Spirit's transforming their lives by filling their hearts with God's love.

We choose to grow in our marriage in the love of God. We are willing to seek Her will. We are willing to do the difficult work of the marriage with the help of the Spirit and in growing more deeply in God's transforming love.

A Blessing
We are here to live virtuous lives from the core or our hearts that are being transformed each day by the Spirit filling us with God's love and mercy.

A Prayer
Open my heart to the presence of the Spirit filling me with the love that honors the covenant with spouses, brothers and sisters in Christ, and with God.

Chapter 18: Don't Pretend it is Easier than it Really Is

"Let's not pretend this is easier than it really is. If you want to live a morally pure life, here's what you have to do. You have to blind your right eye the moment you catch it in a lustful leer. You have to choose to live one-eyed or else be dumped on a moral trash pile. And you have to chop off your right hand the moment you notice it raised threateningly. Better a bloody stomp than your entire being discarded for good in the dump." (5:29-30)

I have attended church all my life. I have heard neither a preacher nor a teacher talk much about living the Christian Life as being difficult. They mostly talked about believing and going to heaven.

The emphasis in churches seems to be primarily on leading the Christian life as leading the moral life, as they define it. Most preachers I have heard in my younger days described the moral life as not drinking alcohol, dancing, or smoking. Today's morality in the church seems to focus on sexual issues of a great variety, the right to carry guns, and getting what we want as long as we do not intend to hurt another.

Most preachers I have heard or hear about living moral lives pick and choose what they consider right morality. Without identifying the passage, most preachers use some of the verses of Romans 1:18-32. This is especially true when preaching about sexual orientation. Have you read this passage in its entirety?

In Romans 1:29-31 Paul lists many immoral behaviors that corrupt the hearts of Jesus' followers and of non-believers. His list includes rampant evil, which is creating chaos and self-centeredness that is destructive to others; grabbing and grasping whatever they want; backstabbing;

envy; wanton killing; bickering; cheating; mean spirited venomous; fork-tonged; bullies; swaggerers; wreckers of lives; insufferable windbags stupid; slimy; cruel; and cold-blooded. And they keep inventing new ways to ruin lives

Take time to read Romans 1:18-32 just to see all the immoral behaviors Paul identifies. However, Christians over-look or disregard all the immoral ways of life that do not seem so bad since they occur every day. Many Christians engage in these immoral behaviors.

He says that it is not that people do not know what they are doing. In our society people may be punished or told-off for doing a few of these things. However, as a culture today we seem to tolerate them more than when I was young. People ignore most of these sins and focus on the individual sins that they disapprove of.

However, I do not find a link between living the moral life that we have created and living the virtuous life Jesus says is given to us by God when we surrender our hearts and minds to what we already have received.

Morality is not the issue for Jesus in this passage or the previous one. In this passage Jesus continues to speak about our virtuous hearts. He was saying that living the Christian life at the core of our beings is very difficult.

It is difficult because we are choosing to consent to God's transforming our way of life that is very different from God's way. Our lives become different from society or culture.

Jesus says in a variety of ways that the way of life of his followers is founded on God's love and mercy. Jesus' life shows when he was the Christ on earth. We are to live this way daily.

God forgave our sins through Christ from when the universe began. He heals us, He gives us hope, and Jesus included the outcasts of his at meals and as his disciples.

The difficulty with living the virtuous life is that it is so different from what we know and what society accepts as acceptable norms. The virtuous heart of Jesus was and is in opposition to values, and accepted standards of churches, culture, and society.

The culture influences of our daily world encourage us to live in ways that center on our comfort and well-being. It says that being self-centered is looking out for ourselves. We are directed by our self-serving egos in how we live and how we relate to others.

Being a Christian is harder than we want it to be. We would rather it requires us only to believe certain doctrines and follow the Ten Commandments. We would rather not have our lives transformed from the inside, making us different from friends, family, neighbors, and others. We don't want to make sacrifices to help the poor, outcasts, family members we don't like and who are not like us.

We may want to down play that Jesus says it is better for us to sacrifice an eye or a hand than to withhold our love from others. We have received God's love and mercy without deserving or earning them. We are to give them to others in the same way.

The Spirit alone can lead us to know what to sacrifice. The Spirit shows us how to sacrifice our image in society to serve the outcast. The Spirit shows us how to use our influence to serve the outcasts and powerless.

We sacrifice the earthly treasures of our right hand in order to live the difficult way and truth of Christ. We sacrifice the eye of earthly values and cultural ways of life.

It is better to sacrifice an eye of material possessions than for a brother or sister in Christ to go hungry or homeless. It is better to sacrifice a hand of influence than for the poor be without enough to sustain their lives and not only to survive.

Let us not pretend that living the Christian life is easier than we want to make it. It is a transformation of our hearts and the total center of our lives.

A Blessing
We are here to follow the narrow and difficult way to share God's love and mercy in the world.

A Prayer
Blessed Christ, lead me to follow your Spirit that I may know the way of your love and mercy to share with those I meet daily.

Chapter 19: Divorce is about Marriage

"Remember the Scripture that says, 'Whoever divorces his wife, let him do it legally, giving her divorce paper and her legal rights'? Too many of you are using that as a cover for selfishness and whim, pretending to be righteous just because you are 'legal.' Please, nor more pretending. If you divorce your wife, you're responsible for making her an adulteress (unless she has already made herself that by sexual promiscuity). And if you marry such a divorced adulteress, you're automatically an adulterer yourself. You can't use legal cover to mask a moral failure." (5:31-32)

This passage appears to be about divorce. I have come to see that underneath the words is an understanding about marriage.

In Jesus' day men could divorce their wives without going to court or having a special reason. A man could give his wife a written notice of divorce and send her away that day. Depending on the man the wife may take nothing with her or he may let her have some possessions. He could send her into the world penniless or give her money or even a business. The husband had all the power.

The women were the losers in divorce. They had no say about the divorce. They could not refute what the husband said. They could not ask for more money or take him to court if he did not pay. Occasionally the wife had money or a business of her own to use after the divorce.

The reality was that women rarely had any place to go after the husband sent them from the marital home. The biological family of a woman would not take her back since she failed in her marriage and was an embarrassment to her family. The divorce was usually considered the woman's fault for not being able to keep their husband.

Jesus is clear that a divorce made a woman an adulteress. Jesus says that if either or both divorced marriage partners remarry they are engaging in an adulterous relationship.

A marriage is two people entering into a marital contract, whether legally registered with a court or made between the two without the involvement of court. They agree to honor, respect, love in all conditions of life, and grow together with one another in the relationship. They commit to become one with each other as they desire to become one with God.

In Jesus' time people may have been more aware of God's involvement with marriage. This would be true even with arranged marriages as was the custom of the day. The parents were expected to be concerned that God was involved in selecting marriage partners. This may not have happened as it was supposed to have. The marriage partners, particularly the husband, may have been more concerned with his wants and desires than God's expectation of a growing intimate relationship between the two.

Divorce means that the couple denies their union and their union with God by having a committed relationship with someone other than their marriage partner. This would also be true if the divorced couple marries others. They have still have not kept their promises to God or to one another.

Selfishness may have been the reality that destroyed the covenant of marriage. Jesus regards a marriage as a sacred union similar to the one with God. Too often marriage partners alienated themselves from Her and no longer do two become one in their relationship.

The couples make a commitment with God, as well as each other. The covenant with God recognizes the joining of two different people to becoming one over the years and in a variety of experiences. It is modeled on the notion of the divergent members of the body of Christ becoming one.

Aren't their exceptions to this point of view? Is the couple to remain in an abusive relationship? Are the couple to remain in a relationship that is not mutual or growing when it is emotional harmful to one or both?

I believe the exception to divorce is when the relationship is not born of God and does not grow in God. God wants none of Her children belittled or physically or emotionally abused.

Let us consider the second significant point of this passage. As I said above, I believe the passage is about marriage more than divorce. A comedian said in the 1960s that the leading reason divorce is marriage. Divorce had reached 50% at that time.

I would alter this 'joke' by saying that the leading reason for divorce is an inadequate understanding of the foundation of marriage. On the one hand people marry because the culture says they should if they are in love. On the other hand, many young people are living together without marrying because they love each other and don't see the need for getting the government involved in their lives. Too often the couple does not make a covenant with one another to become one in heart and mind.

In our culture love is primarily understood as romantic love. Romantic love has more to do with what I want than how two become one in Christ. It is weak in building a marriage on, much less a relationship.

Dr. Karl Barth said that the key in the marriage ceremony is 'whom God has joined together.' Often men and women get married without the foundation of God's love that enables them to withstand the storms in a marital relationship. I believe today we have to look upon divorce differently when marriage does not reflect the community of faith as God intended marriage and family to be.

Dr. Barth also said that marriage is a representation of the body of Christ. We may need to qualify this by saying the body of Christ as found in the teachings of Jesus in particular.

Lasting marriages are built on the foundation of God's love and mercy. Jesus says later in the Sermon that a person can builds her or his house of faith on sand and watch their house be destroyed by the storms of life. They can choose to build their house of faith on rock, which withstand the storms of life.

The same is true for a marriage. The choice by a couple enables the two to build a relationship that grows and endures. They let the couple rejoice and give thanks for one another.

I know that there are times when one or both partners act in destructive ways. They do or say things that challenge the covenant they made. The most difficult part of marriage is forgiving and reconciling.

Forgiveness is difficult to give and to receive. Forgiveness is difficult when one or both partners are hurting and want to lash out. Forgiveness makes our hearts vulnerable when the Spirit is not part of giving the marriage the strength of God's love.

Forgiveness is possible only by letting God's Spirit lead the couple to admit their need for it and their need to give it. The couple must face and answer the question of being willing to let the Spirit lead them to forgiveness.

For most of us reconciliation is even more difficult. We must honestly face the hurts received or inflicted by each partner. A couple has to begin by facing her or his wounds and seek healing through the Spirit.

We must identify and admit our part that led to the hurt or to the destructive behaviors. Outwardly one partner may be primarily responsible. However, a relationship involves two people and usually both contribute to what happens in it.

A seminar leader in marriage counseling helped me understand this. The leader said that there are three personalities in a marriage. There are the two people. The third is the relationship itself. The relationship becomes what the couple makes it, just as each individual becomes who they are because of experiences and influences.

The community of Christ has an important responsibility in marriage. The responsibility is to teach and model God's love and mercy that is the foundation of all relationships. We learn to rely on the presence of God through His Spirit to build a marriage on God's rock of love that withstands the storms and floods of life.

The community of Christ enables us to know how to live with one another even though we are different. We learn from God's presence how the differences can give the marriage joy and strength. We learn how to love with Her love rather than with our ego selfishness.

A Blessing
We are here to live faithfully in God's love in marriage. We invite the Spirit to guide us into nurturing and growing our life together.

A Prayer
O Christ of all relationships, my desire is to be honest and loving in my marriage. I desire the Spirit to lead my marriage to grow deeper and stronger in in your love.

Chapter 20: Manipulating Words to Get Your Way

"And don't say anything you don't mean. This counsel is embedded deep in our traditions. You only make things worse when you lay down a smoke screen of pious talk, saying, 'I'll pray for you,' and never doing it, or saying, 'God be with you,' and not meaning it. You don't make your words true by embellishing them with religious lace. In making your speech sound more religious, it becomes less true. Just say 'yes' and 'no.' When you manipulate words to get your own way, you go wrong." (5:33-37)

All my life I have heard people say, 'I'll pray for you,' or 'You are in my prayers.' Most people respond with gratitude to these promises. They need God's help and trust that the prayers will help. Many say how much difference it made to them during their time of crisis. Yet, how many of us remember to pray regularly for other persons that we have promised to pray for.

The same is true with our saying, 'God be with you during this difficult time.' People like to hear someone say that God is with them and blesses them. They usually feel less alone and assured that they may make it through their crisis. Do we remember to pray for God's presence and how we may be present to the person?

The focus of this passage is being honest. We say what we mean or do not say it if we don't mean it. We are not to say things automatically because that is what one Christian says to another to make the other feel good and have a good image of us.

We may mean what we promise at the time that we will pray for someone or that we wish God's blessings on a person. We may forget our promises. We may forget to pray for God's blessings on them.

To quote a modern day saying: say what we mean and mean what we say. In the Vietnam War soldiers often expressed this by asking if another could walk the talk.

Jesus tells his followers to be truthful in what they say and do what they promise. We are to speak simply and honestly.

Jesus says that a life open to God's transforming love communicates with words that convey our being trustworthy. He says that our words are to be compassionate and honest. This is how God speaks to us.

God's love is still the standard by which we judge what we say to others. In this passage Jesus reminds us that Her love is compassionate, and Her words are trustworthy based on Her compassion.

We discern through the work of the Spirit in our hearts the loving thing to say and how to say it. We open our hearts daily for the Spirit to speak of God's love. We desire to show His love honestly to the world and especially to individuals we make promises to. It is not to say the pious thing because that is what is said in times of crises or joy. We need to give some thought to what we say in the name of God to be sure we are being honest and trustworthy.

The words we speak are not our own. They are God's words. Our words come from our desire for God's love with which the Spirit fills our hearts.

I have not thought until I read this passage about my words speaking God's words to others in the ways Jesus mentions in this passage. Yet, is that not what we are doing? We are using God's promises of love and presence when we say that we will pray for someone or God will bless them. We are speaking out of our experiences of Her love and compassion. Jesus said to his disciples in John last supper discourses that the words he speaks come from God.

We are speaking to a brother or sister in Christ who is hurting or who feels blessed. Jesus tells us to be aware of sharing the pain or joy with another when we promise to pray for them or we speak of God's blessings in their lives.

A Blessing
We are here to speak simply and honestly in compassion, faithfulness, trustworthiness, and love. We are here to speak not for our sakes but for the sake of God's love and the truth of our lives in Christ.

A Prayer
Holy God of love, I desire to say things simply and honestly in your love.

Chapter 21: Live Generously

"Here's another old saying that deserves a second look: 'Eye for eye, tooth for tooth.' Is that going to get us anywhere? Here's what I propose: 'Don't hit back at all.' If someone strikes you, stand there and take it. If someone drags you into court and sues for the shirt off your back, gift wrap your best coat and make a present of it. And if someone takes unfair advantage of you, use the occasion to practice the servant life. No more tit-for-tat stuff. Live generously." (5:38-42)

Jesus says that we are to live generously. Notice that again he refers to an act of compassion as our way of life. The generous way of life that he tells us to live is in contrast and opposition to the cultural way of life based on fear of scarcity.

Jesus says not to hit back if you are struck. That is in opposition to the norms of culture or society. Society teaches that we seek revenge by hitting back because we should not appear weak but prove we will be as strong as the other person, if not stronger.

Jesus also speaks of compassion if someone takes us to court. If they sue us for our best shirt, we should give them out of generosity our best coat. We are to engage no more in 'tit-for-tat stuff.' No more are we to think of revenge or getting even. No more are we to think of how to get back at someone who hurts us physically or economically.

This is very hard to do. Our culture has taught us from our childhood that we don't let anyone get away with doing physical violence to us. Physical violence could be two kids on the playground getting into a tussle and rolling around on the ground hitting each other. It could be two adults becoming mad enough that they exchange punches.

We have seen adults get into fights over politics, sports, and family. I see more adults hitting each other on TV programs, in movies, or in novels than in my daily life.

There are other ways that we can imagine to seek an 'eye for an eye.' In business one contractor undermines another to obtain a contract for a job by speaking half-truths or untruths against a competitor. An 'eye for an eye' would be for the contractor who is undermined does the same thing the next time they are competing for a contract.

A personal example might be when one person becomes very angry with another at church. The angry person tells of a rumor that questions the integrity of the other person so that many beyond the group may hear it. The one belittled by the rumor would find a way to belittle the other person by starting a rumor about the other person.

A person believes his neighbor scratched his car with a key. The angry neighbor gets revenge by missing his turn into his driveway and runs over his neighbor's new, small tree just planted the day before.

I am sure that you can think of other examples. Everyday someone experiences another person undermining a colleague's integrity, or trying to cheat her/him, or gossiping about her or him.

These acts against us make us angry. We want to do something with our anger. What are we do as followers of Jesus to get even?

Jesus says that we do nothing. We do not get even when someone hits us. We do not think of ways of harming the other person when he or she lies about us or misrepresent what we say or do.

Jesus' crucifixion changed an eye for an eye into love and mercy. God did not try to get even with the Romans or the Jews for the crucifixion. God's plan is to say that through the life, death, and resurrection of Christ everything is different in how we relate with one another.

Christians are to be generous with God's love and mercy. Think of all the ways in which God is generous toward us with Her love and mercy. We are far from perfect and have to confess everyday how we have hurt another or have not been compassionate toward others. In God's generosity we are forgiven by Her mercy.

We cannot sustain compassion on our own. We need to rely on the Spirit lead us into compassion and generous way of life for others.

Jesus also gives the example of giving of our best to anyone who sues us in court.

I have never been sued. I can only imagine an example about going to court. The following is a story that I created to give an example of what I believe Jesus means.

What I can imagine is that I borrow a valuable piece of furniture for a party. During the party someone loses his balance and falls on the borrowed piece of furniture. It is broken beyond repair.

When I tell my neighbor, he is enraged. That piece of furniture has been in his family for generations. He says that he thought I'd be more responsible than that. I explain again what happened and he does not want to listen.

A couple of weeks later I receive a summons to court to pay for the destroyed piece of furniture. The amount is more than I have. I tell the neighbor. He says he would see me in court.

On the court date the neighbor's lawyer recounts what happened. My lawyer says I do not have the money to pay for the furniture, but that I could pay a certain amount monthly.

My neighbor refuses. He says that he saw a wall cupboard in my house that he would take as settlement. The cupboard was my mother's and had a lot of sentimental value.

If I understand Jesus correctly, he says to me that I would give the neighbor the cupboard and a sideboard that matches it. The sideboard was also my mother's.

It would cost me a lot in sentiment to part with both pieces. It would cost me to replace them. Yet, Jesus says to me to be generous in love.

My ego would tell me that the neighbor is being unreasonable. My ego would tell me to fight him in court on this. God's ego tells me to give the neighbor a piece of cherished furniture that I have. I do this because my understanding of Christ's way of life is for me to be as generous as God is with me.

This goes against everything that I have learned from culture. Culture would agree with my little ego to find a way to fight the neighbor.

I would be trying to live the generous life God gives me. God's generosity is part of loving and reconciling with others. It is showing love that speaks of forgiveness and reconciliation.

To do this I believe that I must let the Spirit lead me into a deepening, transforming relationship with God. Without a deepening relationship with God, my self-centered ego will run my life. It will undermine my relationship with God. It would block God's love transforming my life to live in His peace and contentment.

A Blessing

We are here to be transformed from seeking retaliation to being loving and showing mercy. We are here to be generous toward those who would seek to get even with us.

A Prayer

O Christ, your strength is in your generosity and gentleness. Teach me to follow you by being generous and gentle and not hitting back. Through your Spirit guide me into ways that loves others and lives generously

Chapter 22: Love Your Enemies

"You're familiar with the old written law, 'Love your friend," and its unwritten companion, 'Hate your enemy.' I'm challenging that. I'm telling you to love your enemies. Let them bring out the best in you, not the worst. When someone gives you a hard time, respond with the energies of prayer, for then you are working out of your true selves, your God-created selves. This is what God does. He gives his best—the sun to warm and the rain to nourish—to everyone, regardless: The good and bad, the nice and nasty. If all you do is love the loveable, do you expect a bonus? Anybody can do that. If you simply say hello to those who greet you, do you expect a medal? Any run-of-the-mill sinner does that." (5:43-47)

What makes a person an enemy? In general, I observe that an enemy is an unfriendly opponent, a military opponent, people hostile toward one another, and people wanting to get even with each other.

Enemies usually avoid one another at church or social gatherings. They usually ignore one another if they meet in public. They will become angry if anyone asks them about each other. They will have only derogatory comments to make about each another.

Politically, there are real enemies who wish to destroy our nation through war, terrorism, or dictatorship of money and/or ideology. There are also persons who are considered enemies because they enter our nation illegally and work to make a better life for their family at home. An enemy could be for some a person of a different culture or religious back ground. There has been an undercurrent in this nation that some people consider African-Americans and women as enemies.

Socially, an enemy may be someone who seeks to make us look bad in the eyes of others to have more esteem. The self-centered ego of one person becomes a rival with the self-centered ego of others when they seek the same job, political office, or dominates a social group. He or she may be someone who gossips or tells lies about others that are entertaining and makes the story teller look good socially. He or she may be someone who engages in a power struggle with us to be have the most influence in a group or in a community.

Religiously, an enemy may be someone who does not believe as we do. I was a pastor at a time when a group from the denomination I belonged to formed their own denomination and told untruths about the denomination they left to persuade others to join them

To be an enemy implies more than not liking someone. It implies more than a short-term antagonistic relationship.

The word enemy implies to me a hostile relationship that has deep roots. We want nothing to do with them. We want to hurt them before they hurt us. Forgiveness usually does not happen between enemies.

When a pastor preached a sermon on this passage, an elder of the church was overheard after the worship service to say that he would never attend that church again if it meant he had to love his enemies.

Jesus says that we are to love our enemies. What may he mean by loving an enemy?

I wonder if 'love' is often misunderstood as Jesus uses it. Love used by Jesus does not mean the same as used by our culture and people in love. It is realistic about others and does not idealize the other persons. God's love accepts a person for who they are and not for who He want them to be. As the love of Jesus was a way of life that changes others, so we are to love others as a way of life.

Seeing an enemy through God's eyes opens our eyes to see them in God's love. He lets the rain fall on the just and the enemies. He lets the draught come to both the just and unjust.

God gives His best to an enemy and a follower of Christ alike. We give our enemies our best when we give them compassion and kindness from our hearts. We offer them forgiveness and seek reconciliation.

We see their imperfection. They may or may not thirst for the living waters of Christ. We see their attempts to hurt us. We strive in love to prevent them from hurting us We pray for the healing of their anger, for their opening their hearts to God, and their letting the Spirit lead them into a life of love.

Christ showed how to love enemies and give them the best that we receive from God's love. Jesus went to the Cross sinless and to give God's best love to all of us that we may be transformed from self-centered to God-centered.

A Blessing
We are here to love our enemies as well as our friends and family. We are here to give our best heart and attitudes to friends and enemies. We are here to pray for our friends and enemies.

A Prayer
Loving God, I desire your Spirit to enable me to love my enemies with your forgiveness and mercy. I desire to give them the best of your love that the Spirit enables me to give.

Chapter 23: You Are Kingdom Citizens

"In a word, what I am saying is *Grow up*. You're kingdom subjects. Now live like it. Live out your God-created identity. Live generously and graciously toward others, the way God lives toward you." (5:48)

Everything Jesus has said to this point he summarizes in the phrase *Grow up*. We hear that a lot as children and teenagers. Some of us hear this in our 20s and 30s. I know some I would like to say it to in their 60s and 70s.

Growing up means taking responsibility for one's life. It means putting away acting childish by playing tricks on others, talking rudely to older people, or breakings streetlights or windows of merchants we don't like. It means accepting the consequences for one's actions and decisions. I am sure that you can add other behaviors that you believe represent a need for a person to grown up.

As we enter our adolescence and 20s, we begin to think for ourselves. We usually look at the information from culture and the church to decide what we will be and what we will not. We begin to behave in ways that we believe are congruent with church teachings and cultural values. We use these ways to develop lives that make sense to us.

In this reflection I have reflected part of what does Jesus mean by 'grow up' in the Christian Life. He reminds us that we grow up within the ways and truth of being members of God's kingdom. We are not lone rangers. We are not isolated Christians figuring out what God wants us to do.

We share with other Christians the study and discussion of being Christian as Jesus was and as the saints of the church have lived through the ages. (By 'saints' I do not mean only those canonized by the church. Paul calls all Christians saints who desire to live as Jesus taught and lived.)

We work for the poor, the powerless, the outcast, the elderly, the disabled, the lonely and grieving, and those in need of medical insurance. We work with other Christians to serve God's kingdom.

We read the tasks of a Christians in Isaiah 61:1-2, among other places. In Psalm 12:5 the Psalmist has God say:

"Into the hovels of the poor,
Into the dark streets where the homeless groan, God speaks:
'I've had enough; I'm on my way
to heal the ache in the heart of the wretched.'"

To grow up as Christians means that we are transformed from living by the values and ways of earthly influences to live by to the values and ways of God's kingdom. We are transformed to live by God's love and mercy, compassion and humility.

Growing up means that we open our hearts to God's presence. We are letting God in. We are consenting to live the way that God has already given us as described by the teachings of the Prophets of Israel, Jesus, and Paul.

We are not our own. We belong to God who created us. We are not individualists. We are part of the body of Christ. We are part of the vast universe that God creates and held together by the love of Christ.

This leads us to the last thing Jesus says about growing up. Out of Christ's love and being part of the body of Christ we live a generous and gracious life.

We do not have eligibility tests to decide who is worthy to receive our generosity or graciousness. God requires us to be compassionate, generous, loving, merciful, kind and gracious to all. She loves us in these ways. We are to love others in the same way.

God's love is not one that has to be earned. God's love is not one that has to meet certain standard to be received. He has no list of requirements we must meet. Love cannot be earned since He makes it present at all time waiting for us to receive it.

To be grown up Christians means that we live the way described in this passage. It does not mean that we decide what we are willing to do to be good Christians, as if God offers us a menu from which we may choose what we like.

The Sermon on the Mount and the scriptures are about how we Grow Up in Christ. The relationship between God's heart and our hearts is important in our growing up in Him. Unless we open our hearts to let the Spirit transform them into a loving and merciful way of life, we cannot grow up in Christ.

We are not asked to work hard at being grown up Christians. We are told that all the ingredients to be grown up Christians are already in our lives. God has put them there. What we have to do is to say "YES" to God to let the Spirit lead us into being Grown Up Christians.

A Blessing

We are here to grow up to be kingdom citizens and to live generously and graciously toward others.

A Prayer

God, you create me to love and show mercy. Christ, you show me how to live God's love and mercy. Spirit, you transform me each day to be more of a kingdom person that a child of selfishness and self-centeredness.

PART II: MATTHEW 6

Chapter 24: Being Good is Not a Performance

"Be especially careful when you are trying to be good so that you don't make a performance out of it. It might be good theater, but the God who made you won't be applauding." (6:1)

Have you ever thought that a good deed you do might be a performance? A 'performance' is what we do for applause from others who see us and from God. A performer seeks recognition and approval, which are expressed by an audience through applause.

One way we perform as children is to raise our hands to answer every question asked by a Sunday school teacher. We answer every question to impress the teacher and class members with our knowledge, whether we are right or wrong. You can tell they are seeking approval when they sit smiling waiting for the teacher to tell them that they are right. They look around the class to see who is smiling at them for knowing the answer.

Some churches put a gold star by a person's name when they attend Sunday school. Many I have known worked hard to have 100% attendance and receive recognition at the end of the Sunday school year by receiving a prize.

The Gospels tell the story of a Pharisee and a Tax Collector (often identified as a Publican) going to the Temple to pray. The Pharisee stands in the center of the crowd there, raises his eyes to heaven, and prays aloud for all to hear. (The significance of raising his eyes is the symbol of looking God in the eye. The tradition of the day was to be more humble by looking down.)

The Pharisee gives thanks for being a religious man who follows God's laws. He especially gives thanks that he is not like the Tax Collector who works to collect taxes for the hated empire of Rome. Tax collectors were among the most hated people and professions in Israel.

The Tax Collector knew how everyone felt about him. He did not stand in the middle of the crowd at the Temple. He stood on the edge of the crowd. He did not raise his head to look God in the eye but bowed his head in humility. He did not tell God how well he keeps the laws and traditions of Israel. He simply asked God to forgive him, a sinner.

He knew that he was a sinner not because he was a tax collector. We don't know if he had a special reason for saying he was a sinner. Perhaps, he was not as faithful to God's laws as he needed to be.

Jesus asked his disciples and the crowd listening to him who went home most blessed. His listeners would likely expect Jesus to say it was the Pharisee because he was such a religious man.

Jesus surprised them. He said that the Tax Collector went home blessed by God. The Pharisee received his favorable recognition for his prayer performance from the crowd. Jesus is clear that the applause from the crowd is all the Pharisee could expect.

God loved the Tax Collector as much as the Pharisee. The Tax Collector prayed humbly to God in a simple and honest way.

The Pharisee did not receive a blessing from God, since he had received his blessing and recognition from the crowd. The Tax Collector wanted God's forgiveness that would change his life.

Jesus says in the early part of the Sermon that his followers must live their faith better than the Pharisees. This parable was an example of what he meant.

He wants his followers to be aware of the faith trap of performance. He wants his followers to be like the humble Tax Collector who places his life in God's hands.

Jesus warns his followers that God does not bless those who perform for the praise of others. Being a good follower of Jesus is to let the Spirit transform our hearts and actions.

Christians are to do good works unnoticed. They are to serve the poor, vulnerable, emotionally wounded, elderly, and physically disabled for the love of God and not praise of her or his follow Christians. If they serve for the recognition of others, Jesus says that they have our reward from other persons and can expect nothing from God.

I was asked once in discussing this verse if I thought a newspaper story about the church helping the poor was an example of performance. The person asking the question noted that such a story highlights for the larger community the needs of the poor.

I agreed that such a story might be helpful. Then I asked what did the article in fact focus on: human good deeds or God's? I asked the group who received the recognition and congratulation. I reminded them of the parable of the Pharisee and the Tax Collector.

Christians live their God-created lives to please God. We serve Him without fanfare or seeking recognition. We do not wait to hear His applause, since there will be none. Jesus refers not to let our right hand know what our left hand is doing.

He and the angels rejoice over our being faithful Christians because of our love for God rather than our striving for public recognition.

A Blessing
We are here to do good for others in response to God's love and not for personal recognition. We serve in quiet ways that only God receives glory.

A Prayer

Merciful God, I desire to have my heart transformed to do loving acts for others in your name and not for our recognition by others.

Chapter 25: Quietly and Unobtrusively

"When you do something for someone else, don't call attention to yourself. You've seen them in action, I am sure— 'play actors' I call them—treating prayer meeting and street corner alike as a stage, acting compassionate as long as someone is watching, playing to the crowds. They get applause, true, but that's all they get. When you help someone out, don't think about how it looks. Just do it— quietly and unobtrusively. That is the way your God, who conceived you in love, working behind the scenes, helps you out. (6:2-4)

This is a continuation of Jesus' teaching in the previous passage. In the first part of Matthew 6 Jesus speaks about living the Christian life only for the sake of sharing God's love and mercy in the world. He emphasizes repeatedly that his followers are not to serve others for applause for a righteous performance. Jesus said in 6:1 that God does not applaud our performances anyway.

We do not do good works to show off that we believe that we are very good Christians. Good works are important, but they are not the same as living the Christian life. We live the Christian life as a natural way of daily life and not for recognition on earth or in heaven.

Jesus says the way that 'play actors' can reestablish their relationship with God is to desire to stop play-acting. They surrender their wills, influenced by their little ego, and willingly let the Spirit lead them to seek Her will. She'll wait for them to open their hearts to Her presence and to humbly seek to live the life of love and mercy that She gives them, even as they are rejecting Her love as the only foundation upon which the Spirit builds their lives.

Jesus says many Christians don't realize that what God looks for is a willingness to open one's heart to the work of the Spirit. He is looking for us to have our hearts transformed from being ego-centered to being filled with His love and mercy. We consent to let the Spirit lead us to surrender the selfish egos in our hearts to be replaced with God's love.

Jesus says that we can't have our cake and eat it too. That is, we cannot work for personal recognition and praise on earth and expect to receive the same recognition from God. When our lives are focused on receiving praise on earth for our good works that is all that we may expect to receive. We cannot expect also to receive from God 'well done, you good and faithful servant.'

Jesus says throughout the Sermon that we do good works because God enables us to do so. God is love by Her nature. The Spirit transform our hearts and lives to be love as we become one with God. We cannot help loving others since our hearts are filled with Her love. We do good works without looking for recognition when we do loving acts toward the physically ill, the chronically ill, the grieving, the mentally ill, the homeless, the hungry, the naked, the lonely, the outcasts, and the strangers. We love Jesus by loving those in need on earth.

A Blessing

We are here to desire humility of heart to live the Christian life. We are here to do the work of God's kingdom quietly and unobtrusively.

A Prayer

Holy Spirit, teach me humility of heart. Fill my heart with God's love and guide me in my work without looking for earthly recognition.

Chapter 26: Prayer is not a Performance

"And when you come before God, don't turn that into a theatrical production either. All these people making a regular show out of their prayers, hoping for stardom! Do you think God sits in a box seat? (6:5)

Prayer is our conversation with God. I was taught as a child that prayer was telling God about my life, my wants, my gratitude, and my desires for the world. I was taught to give a list of my wants to God and wait for Him to answer my prayers.

I am learning that the standard of pray is not what I think or want, but what God wants for the universe and for me. We can use scripture daily to pray with God and hear what God desires for us each day. We find out what God wants in my prayers and actions by reading what Jesus said about God's concern for the lost, wanderers without direction, the outcast of society, and all those who need care from those with the time or money that is needed.

Even our constitution recognizes this when its opening line speaks of 'We the people.' That is important in our society, which so highly values the rights and desire of personal gains of the individual.

The vulnerable and those who suffer from decisions by the wealthy and governing persons who are not shepherds of those in need. Psalm 12:5 is one verse that tells us what and who God is concerned about:

"Into the hovels of the poor,
Into the dark streets where the homeless groan, God
Speaks:
'I've had enough; I'm on my way
to Heal the ache in the heart of the wretched."

I am learning that the most important part of prayer is listening. The Spirit fills our hearts and minds with what God is concerned about. The Spirit leads us to open our hearts to be transformed by God. The Spirit awakens us to what He gives us each day for us to live Her love and mercy.

I read somewhere that the language of God is silence. Prayer is about listening to the Spirit in our hearts and minds. It is consenting to God's presence to lead us to how we may love and served the vulnerable and outcasts. Prayer is about joining God in reconciling the world to Him. Prayer is speaking about God's love, healing, taking care of the most vulnerable, the aged, and for all who persevere with chronic illness.

From scripture and the presence of the Spirit we know what is in God's heart and mind that are to be in ours as well. Jesus joins the prophets and psalmists to say we are to pray by words and deeds for those in economic, physical, emotional, and spiritual need.

So, there is no need for us to put on a performance in our prayers to attract God's attention. She is already present with us. We need only to listen.

I mentioned in an earlier reflection the parable of the Pharisee and the Tax Collector. The parable is a warning about making prayer into a self-centered production. Self-centered prayers probably fall on non-listening ears in heaven. They certainly do not impress God who is not even in our theater of prayer watching our production.

God wants to hear our concerns about our desire to live Her love and the gift of her love for those in need. She wants to know that we share Her concern for refugees, casualties of war, and men and women wanting to earn money to take care of their families in another nation. She weeps over the greedy business and political leaders, liars and cheats, and those who do not admit their sins and need for His mercy. She is concerned for the weak, hungry, naked, ill, imprisoned, and stranger. These are the prayers She hears.

This verse reminds us that the followers of Jesus give glory to God without turning it into a performance that calls attention to themselves. We give thanks for all we have — good or difficult. We open our hearts to receive His love, healing, and mercy in humility and gratitude. The Spirit leads us to know whether our acts of piety are out of His love and mercy or our pretending to be good Christians to receive recognition and applause from others. The Spirit helps us say in solitude in our hearts our surrender to God's love and our gratitude for that love through good times and bad.

We let the Spirit lead us into prayer that is for God's glory and not applause for our performance.

A Blessing
We are here to learn to pray in humility rather than pride. We are here to pray for transformed lives to give daily God's love to all we meet.

A Prayer
Loving Christ, I desire a heart of humility and for your Spirit to lead me to pray for your kingdom to be known on earth as it is in heaven. Teach me to pray with humility rather than arrogance.

Chapter 27: Pray in a Quiet, Secluded Place

"Here's what I want you to do: Find a quiet, secluded place so you won't be tempted to role-play before God. Just be there as simply and honestly as you can manage. The focus will shift from you to God, and you will begin to sense his grace." (6:6)

How do you feel or think about Jesus want us to find a quiet, secluded spot to pray? Remember prayer is not a performance. It is a relationship that begins with God. By God's grace She comes to you do develop a relationship. It is a relationship initiated by God. It is a relationship that we might become one with God and God is one with Christ and the Spirit.

Jesus tells us to find a quiet place that we may listen to God's word in our hearts and minds. The silent place enables us to experience God's words and assuming control of our hearts and minds. He really does not care about our scripts we learn. God cares about our relationship with Him.

We find a secluded place to minimize distractions for us. How can we listen to and experiencing the presence of God with people milling around that we want to impress with our piety?

Jesus says that prayer with God is also to be simple and honest. How is this different from how we pray now? Aren't we honest about want we want God to do? Don't we express our wants of God in simple and honest way?

We probably do pray in simple and honest terms in private. What do we ask for or pray about? Is our focus on what scripture says God wants, or are our words more about what we want for ourselves or for friends and neighbors?

One-way prayer from us to God seems simple. We just use words we learned in church or in books we read. We go through the routine of giving thanks, confessing our sins, praying for others and asking for what we want.

A novel I am reading has a main character whose wife and son died on snowy, slick road. The child lived for a few days after the accident. The father prayed every day for God to spare his son. The child died. The father did not pray for 14 years. He reasoned that if God turned His back of the father's pleading, the father would turn his back on God.

After 14 years he told his story to a woman who had come to mean a lot to him. She trusted God to take care of him. She knew that God may not answer prayers in the way we want, but she was sure She would be present regardless what happened.

After the father told her his story, he sat alone for a while and prayed silently for God's love and peace. He thought at first, He did not answer again. Then he noticed his heart rate lowered, his fist became unclenched, and he felt a peace in his heart. He was surprised that answered could be so simple. He was joyful that he could turn his burden to Him who would heal it and take care of it. The father found his quiet place in the simple way of asking His healing, in the honest way that he surrendered his burden to Him, and in the small manifestation of God's answer to his prayer.

Jesus is also saying that what is important is what God says to us and Her words that we return to Her. Jesus wants us to be in a maturing relationship with God. This is something not emphasized in his day or today. But that is what seems to be his focus.

Silence and solitude enables us to open our hearts to God. It lets us open our hearts to the Spirit to focus on the mystery of God. It helps us to focus on having our hearts and minds filled with His love, mercy, and justice. We often don't know this is what is happening until we emerge from our solitude and live our daily lives.

Silence is necessary for us to quiet our souls (hearts and minds) that we may listen to the Spirit speak God's love to us. Silence means that we are not trying to heal ourselves but are willing to let the Spirit heal the wounds we have.

We are willing to name some of our wounds. Other wounds we have stuffed away to be thought of no more. We did not know what to do with them except get angry or to blame ourselves for something we have done.

God takes a different view of our wounds. Our wounds need the comfort of the loving arms and words of God that gives us peace and wholeness. It may take us a while to surrender ourselves to God believe that God is present and compassionate.

In the silence and solitude, we can know God as the one who is always with us and loves us. God is not waiting to punish us. She is waiting for us to desire the Spirit to lead us to love Her as She already loves us.

Such a God is one we can trust with ourselves. We need not pretend to be better or worse than we are. We can look at our hearts and minds through His eyes and know that He created us and sees us as good. We know that we can risk being honest with Him about our inner most thought and our outer actions without fear of being punished. Most of the time we punish ourselves as we turn away from God and make our decisions apart from His Spirit.

In the silence, we can also speak simply and honestly about others who are hurt or wounded and need God's healing love. She is present to listen to us simply tell our story and pray for others, especially the vulnerable, ill, and grieving. We pray for our world in ways that show our loving concern for all and especially those in storms of war and nature. We also pray for the men and women of power who are in a position to support and protect the vulnerable. We need not use words other than those we use every day. We need only to desire the presence of the Spirit to pray on our behalf.

Jesus tells us in the preceding verses that God is listening for our humility and waiting for our willingness to open our hearts to the work of the Spirit. Those who practice silent prayer for many years may be able to pray silently from their hearts at any time or place. However, they still set aside a time to engage in Centering Prayer or *Lectio Divina*.

In the quiet of a secluded place, what is the point being there unless we are going to keep our words simple? What is the point saying anything unless we are going to be honest? What is the point of having a conversation with the One who knows us better than we know ourselves unless we are going to say what is on our hearts and surrender our will and willingness to God.

It is useless to pretend to be anyone but the person we are. We are to be honest with God about who we are in our egocentricity and arrogance that we have learned over the years. We are to be honest about our fears and our feeling closed off from His love. We are to be honest about our desire for His Spirit and to love others daily. We want to say with Mary. "Yes, I see it all now. I'm the Lord's maid ready to serv3. Let it be with me just as you say." (Luke 1:38)

When we enter God's presence alone, Jesus wants us to come with our hearts open to Her presence. She wants us to bring the truth in our hearts and minds. She is waiting for us to open ourselves to Her love and mercy.

How does this transform our lives? We invite the Spirit to fill our hearts with the love that brings us peace with others and ourselves. We grow deeper in our relationship with God that awaken us to the way of life that unites us with Him.

A Blessing

We are here to talk with God as a friend. We are here to listen to Him in our solitude and silence. We are here to keep our conversation with God simple and honest.

A Prayer:

Abba, you know my heart better than I do. I desire to sit quietly to listen to what you say to me. I desire your Spirit to give me a humble heart and mind to listen to your word and to live by it.

Chapter 28: God Knows Better What We Need

"The world is full of so-called prayer warriors who are prayer-ignorant. They're full of formulas and programs and advice, peddling techniques for getting what you want from God. Don't fall for that nonsense. This is your Father you're dealing with, and he knows better than you what you need." (6:7-8)

I did not know what 'prayer warrior' meant when I first saw it in an email a few years ago. I tried to imagine how followers of the Prince of Peace created it. How could the One who loves us because She is thought of a warrior to attack Her in prayer?

At least that is how I imagined it meant, when I first heard the term. It was explained to me as lot of persons praying to God to make someone well.

I don't know enough to know what outcome the prayer warriors expected. I do know that Jesus says that our prayers should always be that God's will prevail. We cannot overwhelm Him with our prayers for Him to accomplish a specific goal or desire for which we ask. What I read in the gospels is that when we pray we know that God does what is right for us or let us experience life as it is. We pray within God's love that the Spirit says the words for us.

We may have opposing groups praying for God to grant their prayers. Abraham Lincoln said with faithful insight what happens when opposing groups pray for opposing results. In his second inaugural address he said that the people of the North and South prayed to the same God to help them win the Civil War. He observed that neither side had their prayers fully answered.

Lincoln said that both sides had profited from and perpetuated slavery, which is against God's justice. Now both must work together to right this wrong and pay the consequences of helping slaves live free and be integrated into our nation's life. We are aware after 150 years how well that has worked.

This was not easy after 2 centuries of slavery. Many today still oppose the integration of Afro-Americans into our society. They judge the actions of Afro-Americans by the standard of white middle-class society with every understanding that the wounds and scares for both ethnic groups are still prevalent and prevent the two sides from being one nation under God. As a society we have not confessed out sin of keeping Afro-Americans as outcasts and our looking upon them through or prejudice eyes rather than God's all-inclusive eyes.

Today we have many opposing groups praying about a concern. The question in my mind is, what is the loving thing to do for all citizens. The scriptures seem to say that this is the only outcome to pray for.

One thing is sure about prayer. The outcome of prayer is not in our control. Our prayers are to recognize that God controls the results according to His will. Even Jesus said the night of his arrest that His will be done.

How we respond to the outcome of prayer says a lot about our understanding of God. Do we believe that God answers our prayers by meeting our requests? Are we willing to accept God's will when we turn a matter over to Her?

We need to be careful about the programs that offer techniques that promise success in our prayers. These programs too easily lead our little self-centered egos to believe that the right technic assures that God will answer our prayers.

Jesus includes these programs and techniques with other forms of prayer performances. He has already said that God does not respond to performances. He is not impressed with right techniques.

Our little egos and these programs supporting our egos blind us to the reality that God knows what we need. This may be difficult at times when we are invested emotionally, intellectually, or with our public image. Our little egos may believe that they know what is best in our lives and in the world.

Perhaps our prays need to focus on God's love. How do we recognize Her love? How do we love as She desires us to live freely in Her love?

Prayer is about humility and surrender. It is about being silent and being in a place of solitude. It is about speaking with God in simple and honest words about what God is concerned about as revealed in Christ. It is about letting the Spirit fill our hearts and minds with Her concerns. It is about our willingness to follow what He knows we need as the Spirit stirs this reality in our hearts.

With an Abba as we have we need not say much because She already knows. What we do need to say is our love, mercy, compassion, and faithfulness join with Hers daily.

A Blessing

We are here to ask for God's transforming love. We are here to open our hearts to let the love transform us.

A Prayer

God of love, let your Spirit fill my hearts with your love and assurance that you know what I and the world need are your decision and an invitation to me to join you in loving and forgiving.

Chapter 29: Pray Simply, 'Our Father....

"With a God like this loving you, you can pray very simply. Like this: Our Father in heaven, reveal who you are. Set the world right; Do what's best — as above, so below. Keep us alive with three square meals. Keep us forgiven with you and forgiving others. Keep us safe from us and the Devil. You're in charge! You can do anything you want! You're ablaze in beauty! Yes. Yes. Yes." (6:9-13)

Jesus gives us the model of prayer that is not a performance. It also is simple and honest in its wording. It also is concerned about what God is concerned about.

Using this prayer enables us not to be play actors pretending to be pious. We do not let our little egos direct our prayers to be more concerned about our wants and self-concerns. This prayer lets us pray with the simplicity, honesty, and focus on God that Jesus has been emphasizing in the preceding verses.

Jesus begins the prayer with a personal address to God as Abba. (There is a female version of Abba that I will also use: Amma.) Abba/Amma expresses in Aramaic the same relationship that children today express toward their parents using the words Daddy or Mommy.

Abba/Amma invites us to Love Her/Him with the love the Spirit place in our open hearts. We are invited into letting God bring us into unity with Her/Him on earth as Jesus had unity with Her/Him.

The next part of the prayer affirms our desire to live daily in God's will. We ask that Her/His will be done on earth as it is already done in heaven. We want to join in Her/His kingdom on earth with brothers and sisters in Christ. We follow Christ in love, gratuity, showing mercy readily, sharing love, do justice for the vulnerable, and share God's love with all in need of it.

We ask that God make the world right. The prayer recognizes that we are too sinful to know what is right beyond our egocentric natures, much less what is to be done to set the world right. We recognize that God alone has the love and power to make the world right, including making us right.

The prayer next recognizes that we live right by surrendering our will to God and letting the Spirit lead us into holy living. We let the Spirit show us the way to willingly live according to Her/His love, mercy, justice, kindness, compassion, peace, and goodness.

We pray that each day everyone has enough. They need enough clothing, housing, and medical attention. We pray in particular that everyone has enough to eat. Everyone should have enough to enable them to thrive and not only to survive.

This part of the prayer recognizes God's great generosity. He/She gives to all persons not because they deserve anything. He/She gives because He/She is love and cannot help but give abundantly to Her/His children.

We pray to share God's mercy with others. In loving others, we experience the joy and the release from our egocentric bondage through Her/His forgiveness.

We know that we are not perfect and are hurtful to others. We acknowledge that we desire to forgive others and accept forgiveness from others, as God forgives us. We are reminded that unless forgiveness occurs between brothers and sisters in Christ we have no basis for reconciliation with them. This lack of reconciliation puts a wedge between God and us and others and us

Next, we acknowledge the evil in the world. We know the harm of discord and destruction caused by evil. We know the power of evil in our lives that creates chaotic in our hearts and minds.

Yet, at times we do not recognize evil. The harm being done is not seen as harm. It appears as things we agree with. Paul reminds us in Romans that evil pretends to be good and religious. That is why we ask God to protect us from evil with God's love and mercy.

We acknowledge that God alone protects us against the cosmic evil that enters our world and seeks to lure us away from Her/Him. We rely on Her/Him also to save us from evil that leads us to judge ourselves harshly and wrongly. We pray for God's Spirit to lead us out of bondage to evil that makes us self-centered, vengeful, blaming and unloving to others and ourselves.

Our desire is that God's way of love and mercy fills our hearts and directs our lives. This is not an easy way to live. It is possible only when we let the Spirit fills our hearts with God's love and reduced in our hearts our egocentric ways of living.

In light of what we have prayed, the Spirit stirs our hearts with the beauty of God's love, presence, and being in charge. We affirm His caring of the universe and the people of this world. We are filled with His love and joy so that we shout Her/His praise at the end of this prayer. We shout Yes! Yes! Yes!

Blessing

We are here to let Jesus' prayer guide us in simple and honest conversation with God. We are here to be moved by this prayer to live Her/His kingdom on earth as it is in heaven.

A Prayer

O, Christ, I desire that the Spirit keeps this prayer in my heart and to lead us to pray it without ceasing.

Chapter 30: Doing Our Part

"In prayer there is a connection between what God does and what you do. You can't get forgiveness from God, for instance, without also forgiving others. If you refuse to do your part, you cut yourself off from God's part." (6:14-15)

In these two verses Jesus gives us an additional understanding of what our prayers do. Prayer is not only the words exchanged between God and us. Prayer is also the way we live God's love and mercy daily.

Prayer is not something we do to check off an item on our list of spiritual activities. Prayer is the deep concerns of our hearts that match God's concerns.

Jesus is telling us that prayer is connected with our relationship with God and the world. It is connected with our growing up to live the Christian life with the understanding that what we say in quiet times and what we do daily are connected with our relationship with God.

These verses are connected with what Jesus said earlier about being truthful in the words we say to comfort or encourage people when we use phrases such as 'God be with you,' 'I am praying for you,' or 'it is always darkest before the dawn.' These phrases mean nothing unless we follow through with them with our prayers, understanding, support, comfort, and compassion.

In these verses Jesus is going one step further. He says that our relationship with God requires our showing love and mercy toward others. God is saying that if we do not walk our prayer talk we place a barrier in our relationship with God.

Please notice that it is not God who places the barrier between Her and us. We build the barrier. God is always present even when we create a barrier.

God loves us and desires that we open our hearts in prayer that we connect with Her. We open our hearts to let the Spirit lead us into the depth of silence in which we enter Her presence. The Spirit reminds us that God cares for the poor, the powerless, and the stranger in the land. God is also concerned with people grieving and experiencing being wounded by others. God is concerned that the powerful and wealthy take care of those without enough to enable them to thrive in their lives. The Spirit leads us into living the life of Christ that the world may see the kingdom of God on earth.

The example in this passage is about forgiveness. I imagine forgiveness is used by Jesus to make clear our connection with God and the world. God gives us forgiveness, or mercy, to enable us to connect with Him. We are to give forgiveness to others as we are forgiven. Mercy to others is necessary to our connection of reconciliation with others.

Forgiving others is often difficult for us. Forgiveness means that we acknowledge our hurting others and asking forgiveness. It also means that we forgive others in love and are ready to reconcile with those who hurt or do us wrong. It also means that we let the Spirit lead us away from revenge against the other person and leads us to seek reconciliation with her or him instead.

Forgiving another opens our heart to embrace the other person in love. It opens our hearts to be embraced by God in love. Forgiveness frees us from the bondage of anger or thoughts of revenge. We choose to live Christ's way of peacemaking, healing, humility, and willingly to do Her will of reconciling the world unto Herself.

Our part in the power of prayer is the act of extending to others the love and presence that God gives to us. We make real in the world each day the true way of life that God offers to all. We let the Spirit enable us to live for at least for a few moments our true selves that others may see a different way of life from what culture teaches.

What Jesus teaches in the Sermon comes from God. Our part is to live in the paradox of love, which is letting go of controlling the end results and embracing the willingness to do His will. This is not possible to do without desiring God's presence in our hearts made possible through the Spirit.

Doing our part makes us part of the work of the Creator, the Christ, and the Spirit in making the world right. This is part of being the true self that She created us to be. We desire the Spirit to enable us to do our part to make visible God's love and mercy on earth.

A Blessing
We are connected with God through living our prayers, such as forgiving others as God forgives us.

A Prayer
Generous God, I give thanks for your great love that gives me mercy that I may live, move, and have my being in you. Let this love guide my life each day.

Chapter 31: Fasting is not to be a Performance

"When you practice some appetite-denying discipline to better concentrate on God, don't make a production out of it. It might turn you into a small-time celebrity, but it won't make you a saint. If you 'go into training' inwardly, act normal outwardly. Shampoo and comb your hair, brush your teeth, wash your face. God doesn't require attention-getting devices. He won't overlook what you are doing; he'll reward you well." (6:16-18)

The disciple of fasting was a central spiritual practice among the Jews. It became central for Christians as well.

Fasting by Christians for many centuries was primarily during Lent to remind Christians of the crucifixion by not eating meat on Friday. It was a time to remember the death of the old life with the death of Jesus. Once a weak and frighten people following Jesus were reminded through fasting that their new life and commitment was to God alone against whom no power could prevail against his Love.

I learned about fasting on Fridays during Lent from classmates in High School. They would talk about having to eat only fish on Fridays. I had wondered why fish was always served on Friday in the school cafeteria. They also talked about having to give up something during Lent as another discipline.

Most of my classmates did not know the significance of doing those two practices. For them it was a requirement of their church and monitored by their parents. I don't know if the adults related fasting to their faith and relationship with God.

I became aware that with the Protestant Reformation and the diminishing of the discipline of fasting, the meaning became less clear how fasting was related to a person's faith and life. The Protestant churches discussed spiritual discipline very little with some exceptions. Today there are more Protestant churches encouraging and assisting members to include spiritual practices in the growth of their faith and deepening of their relationship with God.

Fasting is one of these practices. It is about stopping for a while habits and practices that we have made central in our lives. Fasting has been broadened in definition from not eating meat on Friday to include anything that we feel we must do to give our lives meaning.

A few years ago, I read a book on fasting by Marjorie Thompson. She discussed other ways to fast to remember the sovereignty of God and His centrality in our lives.

Marjorie Thompson identifies that fasting could include giving up shopping for computers, cell phones, TV and other things that we feel we must have to make our lives more meaningful. She said that we would likely find a stronger sense of meaning that would bring us a lifetime of joy. These material wants have become important to our sense of identity, esteem, wellbeing, and comfort.

We spend the time in prayer or meditation. We seek to remember that God's kingdom has first place in our hearts and not things that we buy or wish we had.

Fasting reminds us that our treasures are in heaven and not on earth. It reminds us to depend on God for all our needs rather than seeking our wants of material things. It reminds us of His generosity and the blessing of our being generous.

Seeking our wellbeing through material goods becomes a problem in our spiritual journey with God when they become more important than our surrendering our will to God. Material goods cannot help us to develop a heart to heart relationship with Her.

Jesus observed in his day people calling attention to themselves when they are fasting. They would dress in ragged clothes, put ashes on their faces and heads, and create solemn faces to show that they were fasting. They wanted everyone to notice their piety by putting on such a performance.

The same temptation of performing for the earthly crowd and God faces us today. We make other people aware that we are fasting from shopping, milk shakes, watching TV, or anything else we are fasting from for a while. We seem unable to avoid turning a spotlight on our piety with words and solemn demeanor.

Here is what Isaiah 58:6-9 says to Israel from God about fasting: "This is the kind of fast day I'm after: to break the chains of injustice, get rid of exploitation in the workplace, free the oppressed, cancel debts. What I'm interested in seeing you do is: sharing your food with the hungry, inviting the homeless poor into your homes, putting clothes on the shivering ill-clad, being available to your own families. Do this and the lights will turn on, and your lives will turn around at once. Your righteousness will pave your way. The God of glory will secure your passage. Then when you pray, God will answer. You'll call out for help and I'll say, 'Here I am.'" (Isaiah 58:6-9)

A Blessing
We are here to fast as a spiritual practice to renew our commitment and deepen our relationship with God.

A Prayer
Loving Christ, show us what we need to fast from and help us to fast and remember your love for us.

Chapter 32: Hearts and Treasures

"Don't hoard treasure down here where it gets eaten by moths and corroded by rust or — worse! — stolen by burglars. Stockpile treasure in heaven, where it's safe from moth and rust and burglars. It's obvious, isn't it? The place where your treasure is is in the place you will most want to be and end up being." (6:19-21)

When I think of material treasures, my first thought is a memory of Treasure Island. I think of treasures as a chest full of jewelry and lots of money. I think of men rushing to claim the treasure before someone else does and about fights over it to determine group gets the treasure.

I am not sure what earthly treasures Jesus was referring to. I imagine he was thinking of what you and I regard as material treasures: such as, heirlooms or expensive possessions, houses, jewelry and clothes, money, investment, etc. Jesus reminds us that what we value on earth will not last: moths ruin clothes; rust eats up uncared for medals; and thieves steal valuable material possessions. These treasures do not give us the lasting pleasure and fulfillment that we desire.

I can't remember having anything that I considered an earthly treasure. I have never had material possession that would leave me heart-broken if I lost it. I might miss a possession, but it would be something that couldn't be replaced. I never had anything of more than ordinary value.

I have known people who have talked about things that they highly value. They have mentioned a family heirloom, a prize bull, an antique car or furniture, or something the accumulation of money or other material possessions that would make them comfortable.

I have the impression that an earthly treasure is highly valued, and the owner protects it with safes and/or alarms. A thief might also consider someone else's possession of great valuable and would want to steal it.

To understand what Jesus is saying we may need to ask ourselves what possession do you own that you paid a lot for or that is a family heirloom that you protect at almost any cost? Do you have something that would leave you heart-broken if you lost it?

It seems that earthly possessions become treasures when their presence gives us a sense of worth and value. Some people believe that their lives are not complete without at least one thing of great value. For some a treasure becomes the center of their lives.

I am not saying they think about it all the time. I am not saying that they build shrines to it or put it in a safe place. I am saying that they value it more highly than anything else.

Jesus reminds us that our earthly treasures that we value greatly are a barrier between God and us. Jesus says that we have to choose what is most important in our lives: our relationship with God or our making earthly possessions central in our lives.

Earthly treasures are barriers to living our true selves. We let them determine our identity. We make them more important than the love of God that the Spirit fills our hearts with.

The loss of earthly treasures can create anxiety. Heavenly treasures are free gifts. Earthly treasures give us pleasures and prestige for the time we are alive. Heavenly treasures give us humility and a God created way of live for eternity.

A heavenly treasure is the love we give to the unlovable. It is the mercy we give to enemies who are in need. It is being realistic about people we know and not try to make them into an illusion of what we want. It is the love and mercy we give on earth.

A heavenly treasure is including outcasts because they are homeless, mentally ill, and ex-convicts. It is recognizing someone wounded and reaching out to them. A heavenly treasure is loving people who are different in their views and sexual orientation.

A heavenly treasure expresses God's love, mercy, and justice. It is about money and possessions being shared with people who are poor, hungry, homeless, etc. It is sacrificing our time to be with the lonely, grieving, and chronically ill.

Heavenly treasures cannot be stolen. They do not rust. We accumulate them as we choose to live the Jesus way and truth. We accumulate them as long as we remember that they are gifts from God and not what we earn. Heavenly treasures are pearls of great price that we give all we have to own.

We desire these treasures to love and be loved by God. Heavenly treasures enable us to desire a heart to heart relationship with Her. Her love leads us to be kind, compassionate, and generous.

Is it easy to use our possessions to feed the hungry, cloth the naked, visit the imprisoned, give medical care to the chronically and temporarily ill, to visit the grieving, or sit with the person suffering with dementia? Too often we develop an attitude of scarcity of love, honor, positions and wealth, believing that we do not grab earthly treasures their will not be enough for me.

No, it is not easy. It is not easy especially when our hearts are attached to earthly treasures. Our egos lead us to desire earthly treasures for our pleasure. The Spirit on the other hand leads us to gather heavenly treasures by serving others and loving the unlovable.

The treasures that we store in heaven are the new heart and mind that God gives us. They are the new God-created way of life in and through Christ.

A Blessing

We are here to store in heaven the treasures of love, mercy, and justice that God gives us, and we let the Spirit guide and give shape to our lives. We are here to use our possessions from God for the least among us.

A Prayer

God of great generosity, I desire your Spirit to instill in my heart and mind your treasures that are eternally stored in you. I want my heart to live with you because my heavenly treasures are with you.

Chapter 33: Eyes are Windows

"Your eyes are windows into your body. If you open your eyes wide in wonder and belief, your body fills with light. If you live squinty-eyed in greed and distrust, your body is a dank cellar. If you pull the blinds on your windows, what a dark life you will have!" (6:22-23)

When I was growing up I spent a lot of time alone because my mother had to work. She spent evenings making her clothes. I did not make friends easily and had none to visit. We lived in places for about a year at a time until I was 12 years old.

T. V. and movies became the source of a lot of my views of the world. Through my eyes entered a make-believe world that seemed real to me. The world that I saw on TV and in the movies became the world that I expected to find beyond. I saw boy gets the girl in a final romantic scene. I saw the bad guys dead at the end of the program.

I came to assume that was what happened in the daily world. When it did not, I waited for it to happen. This make-believe world came into my heart and mind through my eyes. My eyes led me to believe that the make-believe world was the real one.

Jesus says that our eyes have an important part to play in our faith and lives. My eyes did. I did not know how important for many years.

The eyes are the entry point for God's light or for Sin's darkness. The choices we make about what we let in through our eyes influence how we live in the world.

Sin makes our vision narrow so that we see more darkness than light. Sin does not want us to see through God's eyes the reality God's world that transforms our lives. Sin lets in the darkness of the self-centered egos. We see and judge negatively those who are different, outcasts, vulnerable, or in need. We don't see them as our brothers and sisters in Christ.

The term squinty-eyes reminds me of people similar to Scrooge. Their eyes let in only the view of whether others want his money, rather than work and save as he did. They seem to look for things that they can judge as wrong, bad, unworthy, etc. They see the world with a negative attitude about and toward others.

They are satisfied with their lives. Their vision sees no reason to have more than they do or to help those with less money or possessions rise to thriving rather than only surviving. They are not interested in a positive outlook.

They have closed their hearts to the work of the Spirit. They have no interest in having their hearts filled with God's love and mercy. They do not consent to see others through God's eyes, rather than only through their eyes.

The Spirit can lead us to choose to open our eyes wide to let in God's light. We look at the world with joy and gratitude with eyes full of love and wonder. Wide-open eyes come from our relationship with Him.

Looking at the world through God's eyes is not idealizing the world. It is not pretending that everyone is content and growing in wealth and possession. It is not pretending that everyone is kind and well intentioned. We look at the world through the eyes of the Creator who sees the reality of creating Adam to tend His world and then having to evict him from the Garden.

We desire God's Spirit to enable us to see the world through God's love and mercy. We open our hearts to see Her wonders and to let in the light of Her presence. She leads us to the center of God's loving heart that we may see the real world and not the one we create out of the squinty eyes of darkness.

We make a choice to live in darkness or to let the Spirit open our eyes wide to God's light that the darkness can never overcome. It is a true and certain reality that His love and light keep our eyes wide open to see the world as it really is.

A Blessing
We are here to be wide-eyed to the wonders of God's universe created and sustained by love. We are here to let the Spirit open our eyes to Her presence and gift of new life and light.

A Prayer
God of wonder, I desire your Spirit to open my squinty-eyes that lets in more darkness than light. I desire to see with joy and thanksgiving the light of your presence.

Chapter 34: We Cannot Serve God and Our Egos

"You can't worship two gods at once. Loving one god, you'll end up hating the other. Adoration of one feeds contempt for the other. You can't worship God and Money both." **(6:24)**

This verse is one of the few verses in which Jesus is giving his followers an either/or choice. The reality is that we cannot give our whole hearts to two opposing loyalties to influence our lives and giving meaning to us.

Some people today believe that they can serve to two gods equally. They give loyalty to cultural values during the week and to church on week-ends, unless there is a little league for their children or a pro football game.

I remember reading awhile back some research that may show that this is not possible. The scientists discovered that there is a section of our brains that produce love at first sight that is deep and exclusive in nature. That part of the brain also draws people together who are physically or emotionally intimate even when they would deny that that is happening. The attraction between the two is what makes it difficult for one or both parties to end the relationship.

The author of the article says that because of this finding he has come to believe that there is no such thing as casual sex. During sex this part of the brain is activated that draws the partners close together. One or both may say that they are just having physical sex that they can stop at any time. However, given the findings, this part of the brain creates a form of strong attraction between the two. The author found that the part of the brain that stimulates attractions between two people is very near the part of the brain that stimulates addictions to a variety of thing include drugs and alcohol.

This scientific finding does give some validity to what Jesus is saying. We may be attracted to two gods but cannot give our whole self to both. At times we give ourselves to neither. We cannot give our heart or loyalty to God and Money or positions or anything else. The kind of loyalty about which Jesus speaks is lodged in our hearts and directs our lives regardless of what we may say.

We may not realize that we are giving Money control in our lives. Our minds usually tell us that there is no contradiction worshipping God and pursuing the benefits and entitlements of earthly treasures. However, Jesus says throughout his teachings that the kingdom of God or the entitlements of Money are opposed to each other.

Money is likely a metaphor for the earthly treasures that we accumulate. Money includes all of our material possessions. Money also refers to any habit or addiction that primarily influence our values and way of life other than God.

Money is a metaphor for egocentric living. Our little egos encourage us to acquire possessions that satisfy our desire for well-being and feeling worthwhile as persons. These possessions also are intended to enhance our self-image. They give us a sense of personal power, influence, security, or esteem.

Here are a couple of illustrations to illustrate what I mean. Our little egos encourage us to buy a $50,000 automobile when we can meet our need with one costing $25,000. We buy an $800,000 house when a $400,000 one will be comfortable. Our egos persuade us that we go on expensive vacations when one that is half the cost gives us what we need.

What makes these choices a worship of Money? We are making choices for our benefit and not for sharing with those with less. For us to sacrifice what our money will by that is more expensive, we spend less and share the difference so that the least can thrive more than survive. We have in our nation a large number of people, mainly children, who do not have enough to survive on. The families struggle to survive each day and want a job but have no transportation; have little education or work experience; cannot find affordable child care; and must depend on the government and charities for what helps them survive.

An irony I experienced in the 1970s recession. Middle class people lost their job and needed to feed their families. They applied for Food Stamps. They were incensed by the questions they were asked because they believed the questions were intrusive in their lives. They did not like how they were treated in applying for food stamps, which barely fed their family.

This is an important example because it tells us what intrusive interviews millions of American citizens must go through to feed, shelter, and clothe their families. Too often they are looked down upon because they are asking for assistance and are treated as less than children of God.

To worship God and Money also means that we believe we can have an intimate relationship with God while pursuing a life-style that uses our money each month for our self-interest. Our little egos also want us to believe that we need not worry about the needy, vulnerable, and outcasts just because God does. Since God is concerned with them they will be taken care of somehow. Our little egos tell us to look after ourselves first and let some do-gooders took after the poor.

When we seek God's presence and open our hearts to God's Spirit, the Spirit works in our hearts guiding us to know the difference between what we want and what we need. God gives us what we need that She knows is right for us. The Spirit guides us to do for the other persons giving what they need to live and not only to survive.

Money conflicts with God when our egos convince us to use it to serve our wants first and then we help people at Thanksgiving and Christmas. There is no conflict when our lives are Christ centered, showing God's kingdom on earth.

If we give first loyalty to Money or our little egos, we are going to look at all of life through the lens of earning lots of money for our personal wants. If we give our first loyalty to God, we are willing to be self-giving for the sake of others.

We eventually have to choose between God and Money because it is impossible to live with more than one primary commitment when the two oppose each other. When anxiety over earthly possessions and money fills our hearts, it does not leave room in our hearts to love Her and others. When we choose Her as our primary commitment, the possession and use of money is transformed to serve Her kingdom on earth that reflects Her love for the entire universe.

A Blessing

We are here to give God the first and only place in our hearts. We are here to use our earthly treasures to serve others according to Her love and generosity.

A Prayer

Loving Spirit, lead me to live generously with earthly possessions, as God is generous with me. Lead me to keep money in its rightful perspective in light of God's love and mercy.

Chapter 35: Life of God-Worship

"If you decide for God, living a life of God-worship, it follows that you don't fuss about what's on the table at mealtimes or whether the clothes in your closet are in fashion. There is far more to your life than the food you put in your stomach, more to your outer appearance than the clothes you hang on your body. Look at the birds, free and unfettered not tied down to a job description, careless in the care of God. And you count far more to him than birds." (6:25-26)

Trust is a difficult issue for many of us. Distrust comes when a confidence is betrayed that we share with another person whom we trusted. We do not trust that person again. We may wonder if we can trust anyone with our confidences or what they tell us.

I heard a speaker say that the hardest person to trust is our self. Trusting our self is difficult when we doubt that we are able to do what we are asked to do but try anyway in order not to disappoint another. We may fear the punitive consequences of failing. We may not trust that we are good at making a speech, making a positive impression in a job interview, or trying something new.

An example of the latter is when I learned that our dog has diabetes. This involved giving him a shot twice a day. I did not trust that I could learn how to do this without hurting the dog. It did not help that when I was practicing give a shot at the veterinarian's the dog nipped me.

I initially said that I would not give the shots because I did not trust myself. Now I give his shots without his flinching or growling at me. Even if he does, I trust myself enough to give him the shot.

To trust others and ourselves means that we trust that we are stilled love by others and can continue to love ourselves. It means to do a task when we doubt ourselves. It means asking for help until we learn how to do the task. It means knowing ourselves well enough to be able to say 'no' if we know we do not have the skills to do a task.

Jesus says that when we choose God-worship we can trust our lives with God as does the birds. God gives birds their feathers to help them fly and to protect them from the weather. God provides food when they need it.

We are more important than the birds. God's love is still present in our trust and distrust. Her love is present in the midst of our worry over having enough food and the right clothes to make a good impression.

Jesus reminds us that our lives are more than what we eat or the image we make without clothes. It is more than working hard to be sure that we provide family with food, shelter, and clothing. Too often our worry over money keeps us in a job that does not suit us. It closes our hearts to the work of the Spirit to trust all of our life to God.

Jesus says that trust in God can lead us to answer Her call and provide what our family needs. He is telling us what we can trust our daily living to God because He knows what is right for us. Think of how God can make a difficult job better by giving us the Spirit to join and guide us in doing it.

Imagine what it might be like to trust that God would help us have joy in the work we do. Imagine trusting Him to lead us to live the spiritual gifts of goodness, self-control, kindness, compassion, and love in the job we have.

Imagine using your gifts as best you can. Imagine that you know in our heart what Paul says of being content in whatever circumstances he finds himself.

Not everyone in Jesus' day or today is ready to follow him in this way. They lack trust in the One they cannot see. They are not sure in their hearts that God knows better than they do what is right for them. They may have experienced praying to God who does not answer their prayer the way they expect.

To be a God-worshipper completely changes our lives. We commit to a deepening love and friendship with God. God-worship is about a way of life in which we desire the Spirit to help us grow into that our trust is in God is growing deeper.

Jesus says that trust in and love of God diminishes worries as the Spirit transforms our hearts and minds. God feeds our hearts with His love, as we open our hearts to and desire His presence.

God's love nourishes us with the satisfying bread that Jesus said is his body. It fills us with the living waters that satisfy our thirst to be loved for our imperfect selves. It gives us the wine to remember our true life in his blood. It enables us to say more often that it is not I who live but Christ who lives within me.

A Blessing

We are here to trust and love God to be the foundation upon which the Spirit builds our faith and life. We are here to trust that God will provide what we need

A Prayer

Loving God, it is not easy to trust. I have been disappointed often in my life in trusting others and myself. I desire for your Spirit to lead me into a life of God-worship that trusts in you alone.

Chapter 36: Living Simply

"Has anyone by fussing in front of the mirror ever gotten taller by so much as an inch? All the time and money wasted on fashion—do you think it makes that much difference? Instead of looking at the fashions, walk out into the fields and look at the wildflowers. They never primp or shop, but have you ever seen color and design quite like it? The ten best-dressed men and women in the country look shabby alongside them." (6:27-29)

This is another way of looking at the question of who we trust with our daily lives and relationships: God or Money. As we said in an earlier chapter, the definition of Money needs to be understood broader than coins and paper bills we call money. It includes our egos that are concerned with possessions of all kinds: such as houses, cars, clothes, organizational offices we may hold, and other things that will impress others with the quality of our possessions. Money is considered a god when we use our possessions for ourselves and do not share regularly with those who struggle to survive.

Physical earthly images are not as important to our heart to heart relationship with God as quiet, solitude, truth, and honesty. The beauty of faithful living is found in contemplation by opening our hearts to God's presence and to serve God's children, who are emotionally or physically disabled, or who are the poor and outcasts.

Does the beauty of our faith come from our earthly image created by clothing, housing, automobiles, jobs, or club membership? Is a loving heart from God to strive to be one of the 10 best-dressed people?

There are people who want the power, influence, esteem, and possessions to have the image and status that people admire and give power to. God gives us possessions as gifts to be used for the well-being of others.

Many people give great value to the message from advertisers and society that a good outward impression makes a good first impression. We may believe that such a good impression is likely to lead to having many earthly treasures of esteem or high paying employment.

Jesus says that no one has ever gained success by worrying about her or his self-image. Using a variety of products promising to make us more youthful and more attractive have nothing to do with our life of faith and our hearts and minds being filled with God's love and mercy.

It is not easy to be content with our God-created image of goodness, patience, kindness, generosity, friendship, love, compassion, and simplicity. These things are not valued in the earthly way of creating a good image.

St. Therese of Lisieux said on her deathbed that she goes to God with empty hands. She takes to God no earthly created personal image or works of righteousness. She takes only herself and Jesus' love for her and her love for him. Her self-image is a gift from God and not something that she created. She trusts God with her whole heart to love and accept her as she is.

This is the basic way of living a simple life. We need not accumulate a lot of things just because we like them or may want them some day and can afford them. We need not live in an impressive house or have impressive furniture.

We need to desire the Spirit to be present in our hearts to fill them with God's love. God's love and presence is the foundation for our trust in God to care for our needs and knowing what is right for us. We remember that all that we have and all we are come from Her. These are what are important in our relationship with Her. This is how we learn about the simple way of a Christian life.

A Blessing

We are here to be beautiful through God's love and gift of our true selves. We are here to walk humbly with Him that we may learn how to live simply in His love. We are here to see and delight in the simple life that He gives us through Christ.

A Prayer

Brother Christ, my eyes too often become clouded by the false glamor of the world. I desire your Spirit to open my eyes to the beautiful and simple life you give me in your presence.

Chapter 37: God Meets Everyday Human Concerns

"If God gives such attention to the appearance of wildflowers—most of which are never even seen-don't you think he'll attend to you, take pride in you, do his best for you? What I'm trying to do here is to get you to relax, to not be so preoccupied with getting, so you can respond to God's giving. People who don't know God and the way he works fuss over these things, but you know both God and how he works. Steep your life in God-reality, God-initiative, and God-provisions. Don't worry about missing out. You'll find all your everyday human concerns will be met." (6:30-33)

I am reminded of a story that happened to a friend of mine. She had the unexpected thought of going on a pilgrimage to the cathedrals of Paris. She had not thought before about going on such a pilgrimage. She decided that this was from God, since it was so unexpected and was intended to deepen her faith.

She planned a pilgrimage that would visit as many of the cathedrals of the city as her time allowed. She did not know what she was to find. She did not know if she would afford to go. Yet, if the pilgrimage was from God, God would show her the way.

She saved her money over several weeks. The time came when enough money was saved. She was ready to go.

Two or three weeks before she was to leave her car had to be repaired. She had to have her car repair to do her job. Then a friend of hers had a financial emergency. She felt led to give her friend the money she needed.

She spent all the money she had saved for her pilgrimage. She told me that she was disappointed. She said that she resigned herself to not being able to go. She decided that the pilgrimage was her idea and not God's.

She shared her disappointment with another friend. The friend said she had some extra money and gave her a donation.

A couple of other gifts came that provided all the money she needed and more for the trip. When she told me her story, she was within a week of leaving.

Telling me the story brought tears of gratitude to her eyes. She discerned that God was teaching her to trust His love and care.

When she returned, she told me of encounters in the cathedrals and the people she met that she felt were gifts from God. She said that being in the cathedrals for times of meditation and wonder gave her a closer sense in her heart of God's presence.

When she spent the money that she had initially saved for her trip, she could have become preoccupied with her disappointment of not going. She could have become preoccupied with wondering why this happened to her when she was so sure going on the trip came from God.

She did none of these. She said that the use of her money for her car was a necessity. Helping her friend was a strong sense of God's will. She knew she had been right in how she used her trip savings.

She said that in the midst of her disappointment she was aware of the sense that if her trip were of God's plan, it would happen. Her relationship with God gave her trust in God taking care of her in ways right for her. She did not become preoccupied with disappointment, doubts, or confusion about not going.

She recognized the subsequent donations from friends were from God. The donations were not only gifts of money they were gifts of community. God was saying that we grow spiritually in the body of Christ from the love of brothers and sisters in Christ.

She was relaxing as Jesus says so that she could respond to the gifts. The gifts were from God's generosity. She found that her trust in God grew.

Looking back on the story I am reminded of the story of Abraham and Isaac. God tested Abraham's faith by asking him to sacrifice Isaac. He was asking Abraham to let go of promises made with the birth of Isaac.

My friend's faith was also tested. God asked her to sacrifice her trip that she believed was a promise from God for her spiritual nourishment.

In both stories God provided the means for fulfilling the promises. She gave Abraham a lamb to sacrifice instead of Isaac. She gave my friends a community that enabled her to go on pilgrim rather than using her savings, which would have been her doing rather than God's gift through her community of faith.

God gives us many opportunities to relax and rely on His presence and love when we open our hearts to Him and the leading of the Spirit. He teaches us to let go of relying on the fulfillment of promises, even from Her. She teaches us to rely on Her to know what is right for us and to do what is right for us. She teaches us the relationship of Her love.

My experiences have been very similar. I usually have to be willing to give up what I want. That is because too often what I work to have is relying on myself and not God. If I am to be faithful to trust God's love and mercy, I have to be willing to trust not my will and way, but God's.

A Blessing

We are here to make preoccupations with our lives less important than our love from and for God. We are here to relax into God and receive the gifts from Her than we need and are right for us.

A Prayer

Loving God, I desire your Spirit to lead me to see life through your reality and relax in a simple life that comes from trust in you.

Chapter 38: Living in the Present

"Give your entire attention to what God is doing right now, and don't get worked up about what may or may not happen tomorrow. God will help you deal with whatever hard things come up when the time comes." (6:34)

I am not exactly sure where I learned to worry. I think it was from my mother. I can remember worrying about many things. Of course, since we had just enough to rent a room, eat, lay-away my clothes, and pay charge accounts, I imagine worrying was a normal part of life.

Of course, worrying got neither of us what we worried about. I rarely knew what my mother worried about. I worried because I thought my mother worried. In the long run we relied on what mother could figure out. I trust that God looked upon us and helped us with whatever we were worrying about.

I spent a lot of time during my life wondering what I might have done differently or better in the past. I especially worried whether I was behaving and carrying out tasks in ways that mother approved.

I remember hearing sermons when I was growing up about what God is doing now to save me to go to heaven. I do not remember sermons about God's knowing what is right for me and that Her love will always take care of me. I am not sure I ever heard in church that the Spirit of God is always present with me and takes care of my worries and me.

Have you ever noticed how worry affects your mood and thinking? Worry is an uncertainty about our present and future. It is feeling that bad things will happen, and no one is there to help us.

For three years I worked at a community mental health center. I began to notice that most of my clients and my colleagues focused on what happened wrong in the past and how they will do better in the future. It took many sessions with my clients before some of them began to look at what can be done today to help their wounds often made worse by unfounded worry begin to heal.

They did not spend much time thinking or talking about the present. They did not ask what needed to happen today to find healing that enabled them to live in peace and love with their illness.

Have you heard the saying, as I have most of my life, that the past is gone except what we cling to in our minds and hearts? Tomorrow has yet to come and we do not know what may happen. Today is what is actually all we have in which to live.

I have heard that saying but I have spent most of my life ignoring it. I really did not understand what it was trying to tell me until a few years ago.

I spent too much time wondering if I did the right thing in the past. I wonder if I am going to do and say what God wants me to. I have spent so much time looking back or ahead that I had little or no time to let the Spirit guide me today. Most of the past does not matter anyway since it is gone. The future does not matter since it has not yet arrived.

Today matters most. What we did in the past may influence today. What we do today may influence tomorrow. However, we have only today in which to live differently from the past and lay the foundation for the future. Jesus tells us that we must choose to whom we surrender our lives. What matters is our desire primarily to trust in God or to trust in ourselves.

What is the connection of the past and present? The present is created by the decisions we made in the past. Once we have made them we cannot undo them. We can however learn from the past without worrying about it. We can learn to live differently in the present.

The future and the present are connected by what we decide today, which influences our lives in the future. We can worry about whether we are doing the right things now so that our future will be good and bright. But there are no guarantees since other things can influence the future: such as getting married, a job, moving, death in the family, or friendships

Jesus tells us that worry does not solve a problem. He says that the alternative to worrying is to focus our attention on what God is doing in our lives today.

God invites us to let the Spirit lead us to trust both His love and mercy in the present. I am discovering that this means surrendering daily my worrying. Worry is my trying to control my life instead of surrendering to the Spirit. It means to let the Spirit lead me to trust God's mercy in the past and His love in the future.

Paul says something similar as Jesus in I Corinthians 10:13, "No test or temptation that comes your way is beyond the course of what others have to face. *All you need to remember is that God will never let you down, he'll never let you be pushed past your limit; he'll always be there to help you come through it.*" (my emphasis)

God is always present with us. We can be grateful for what we have received so far in our lives from Her to help us face the unknowns and the difficult issues in our lives. Her mercy enables us to accept the forgiveness we need for some of our past.

We can face with confidence today or tomorrow trusting the presence of God's Spirit in our hearts and minds. We can do this with relaxed certainty in the midst of our anxiety.

After all, we are God's children. God knows better what is right for us than anyone else or us. As we said earlier, trusting God is the most difficult act of faith we have. Yet, it is the only act of faith that enables us to live today and not yesterday or tomorrow.

A Blessing

We are here to put our trust in God's loving presence to be with Her each day and to surrender to Her will today. We are here to turn our worrying about tomorrow over to Her. We are here to let Her mercy redeem our past to remember no more.

A Prayer

Ever-present God, my heart is full of gratitude that you are in my life today. I desire to let you Spirit lead me to live in trust of you each moment of my life.

PART III: MATTHEW 7

Chapter 39: Don't Pick on People

"Don't pick on people, jump on their failures, criticize their faults—unless, of course, you want the same treatment. That critical spirit has a way of boomeranging. It's easy to see a smudge on your neighbor's face and be oblivious to the ugly sneer on your own. Do you have the nerve to say, 'Let me wash your face for you,' when your own face is distorted by contempt? It's this whole traveling road-show mentality all over again, playing a holier-than-thou part instead of just living your part. Wipe that ugly sneer off your won face, and you might be fit to offer a washcloth to your neighbor." (7:1-5)

I heard a story that may illustrate this passage. A woman over 80 was very critical about others.

She was not a mean person. She did not think of herself as being critical. She was not aware that others thought of her as being critical.

She thought that she was pointing out obvious imperfections of another person. She parroted the criticisms of her that she heard growing up.

She did not think about her similar imperfections. She was overweight. She had trouble reading part of the lesson in Sunday school. She criticized the official board of the church but refused to be part of it. She criticized elected officials but had no solutions except the current ones that did not work to her liking.

She could see with clear vision the smudge on the face of another person. She could not see that her criticism often caused her face to become distorted with a scowl or frown.

Unfortunately for her, she experienced a couple of strokes a few months a part. The second stroke left her unable to say the words that she intended to say, such as her referring to a group of high school student as carrying skateboards when they were carrying backpacks.

After her second stroke she had become kind and compassionate. She was able to express her love in positive ways. She still had her moments of criticism toward strangers, but she spoke more lovingly toward her family.

The point Jesus is making is that criticism of any kind is not an expression of God's love and mercy. God is not impressed with our pointing out the mistakes of others while ignoring our own. Others can see the disapproval on the face of a critical person or hear it in her or his voice.

What we do in focusing on the smudge of others and ignoring our distorted face is to close our hearts to God and the person we are criticizing. We no longer see them through God's eyes. We no longer consider in our hearts that the other person is His child, created in His image. We also ignore that as a child of God we are to be kind and compassionate, as God is toward us.

Such criticism makes it difficult for us to be kind, just, compassionate, or loving. We close our hearts to the work of the Spirit to fill our hearts with love and mercy. We turn our hearts from growing deeper in love with Her. We do not let the Spirit transform our hearts to live the Jesus way rather than the self-centered way of our little egos.

God's love does not mean that we ignore the reality of another person. We do not ignore their weight, their clothes, or their opinions. Those things no longer matter in how we relate to them. We love the person because the other things don't matter when we love another child of God.

We embrace them in love. We open our hearts to be embraced by them. We open our lives to be embraced by God's love and to let the Spirit lead us into a new life that enables God's love to transform our critical selves and distorted face. We see the smudge on the face of another with compassion and humble desire to be God's means of cleaning or healing it. God's love is in the midst of our lives and the Spirit leads us to love the other with God's love.

We rejoice in God's love. We rejoice in giving God's love. We rejoice in receiving God's love from others. We rejoice in humility rather than being right.

We have no need to pick on others.

A Blessing

We are here to love one another in kindness, humility, goodness, and gentleness. We are here to be honest about our critical attitudes and love for others.

Prayer

I desire, loving God, for your Spirit to transform my critical heart and tongue. I desire to be honest about my critical self. I desire that the Spirit lead me into a daily life of humility and love.

Chapter 40: Don't be Flip with the Sacred

"Don't be flip with the sacred. Banter and silliness give no honor to God. Don't reduce holy mysteries to slogans. In trying to be relevant, you're only being cute and inviting sacrilege." (7:6)

I don't hear the word 'flip' used very often today. as much I did when growing up. Then flip meant making fun of something, not taking something seriously, or not consider what someone said as having little importance. It referred to being dismissive, jesting, offhanded, jokey, unserious, or lighthearted.

I have tried to think of ways that I have heard people being flippant about God, the sacraments, salvation, worship, Jesus, the cross, resurrection, the work of the church, etc. I have heard a few people trying to be cute or sarcastic about something in scripture to show that faith is not serious for them anymore.

What I have heard or seen more often is the use of slogans to get people's attention about what a church says about its life and faith. I have seen a church's message reduce the gospel or faith to slogans.

One that I remember is 'do you know where you will spend eternity?' We do not have the final say in whether we live in God beyond the grave. We do take part in this decision by whether we desire God's love in our hearts and desire the Spirit to help us live Her love daily on this side of the grave.

I have heard of worship services and church programs that are intended to be relevant and appeal to the younger generation. Live bands and orders of worship shown on a screen sound relevant to a new generation. Coming to worship in casual clothes is thought to be more appealing to adults under 40 years of age.

I read a theologian saying that the church committed to Christ will survive only if members follow the path of contemplation. This path leads to a more intimate relationship with God and one another. It also leads to living God's kingdom.

God is concerned with those who are powerless, considered outsiders, and vulnerable such as the elderly and children. I have read other contemplatives say that the emerging church must emphasize the Contemplative life to be relevant to its call to be God's kingdom on earth.

Our commitment to Jesus is to let God transform our lives through Her love, mercy, and presence. The transformation fills our hearts and lives with the spiritual ways listed in Galatians 5:22-23 and the beatitudes found in Matthew 5. We cannot transform ourselves by our will power. We must desire the Spirit of God and Christ to lead us in the ways of transformed life.

What is relevant in worship is being encouraged to live the Christian Life based on God's love. Relevant worship leads us to desire the Spirit to guide us to live God's love through the week. It leads us to take time each day to let the Spirit open our hearts to be filled with God's love. I have come to see the Contemplative approach to worship as doing this most consistently. How this is done may vary. That it is done is necessary to have God's strength and love to live daily.

We may have spent too many centuries emphasizing the Christian faith as a way of knowing about God or faith based primarily on intellect and ideology. We know about God through the catechisms. We know about Jesus through the biblical verses we learn. We know about the Christian life through the moralisms that are given to us. None of these lead us to know Him in a relationship that grows in our hearts and daily lives.

Worship is an example of the difference between knowing about the gospel and living it. The Spirit can use worship with our consent and desire to lead us into a deeper relationship with God. Worship shapes our lives as Christians. For worship to last through the week we need to let the Spirit enter our hearts to fill them with God's love and mercy, as well as God's word each week and each day. Worship is an important place for this to happen to us.

Important also is our individual time of solitude and silence outside of corporate worship. This is the time each day we spend letting the Spirit awaken our hearts and minds to be embraced by God's presence. It is the time to let the Spirit lead us to know better how we are to live the Christian life during each day of the week.

What we know about the Gospel is important. How we live the Gospel is more important. Becoming one with God is the grace that we receive from God's Spirit.

A Blessing
We are here to make the church relevant by being the church Christ called into being.

A Prayer
Merciful God, open my eyes to the live the ways of faith that are not flippant with your love and mercy

Chapter 41: Be Direct

"Don't bargain with God. Be direct. Ask for what you need. This isn't a cat-and-mouse, hide-and-seek game we're in. If your child asks for bread, do you trick him with sawdust? If he asks for fish, do you scare him with a live snake on his plate? As bad as you are, you wouldn't think of such a thing. You're at least decent to your own children. So don't you think the God who conceived you in love will be even better?" (7:7-11)

God does not give us what we want. Our wants usually focus on our desires that give us a good image, nice possessions, or personal power. God gives us what we need for our relationship with Him. He gives us what we need to be compassionate, faithful, prayerful, good, generous, firm in the faith, and loyal to following Christ.

What we want is usually what will benefit us. We want to win a tournament, score a run or a goal, receive admiring looks for our new clothes or care, and to have influence to control a group the way we think it ought to be.

I imagine that you can name other things that you want to satisfy your longings for earthly treasures or give you pleasure. Often having new things or being well liked has to do with one's image in society.

We often bargain with God to receive what we want. We promise to act better or attend church more. I have heard teenagers promise to study more if God will rescue them this one time on a text. I have heard adults promise to attend worship more or to be more kind to people they do not like if they could get a promotion or win the lottery.

God does not bargain. She does not give us what we want to make us happy or to keep our prestige up. God looks to what we need for a better relationship with Her in our hearts and minds, and with others in business, family, or where one lives.

God will not be manipulated. We may think that we can manipulate Him by promising to give more of our time or money to the church. We may think that we can manipulate Him by promising to pray more often, praise His more, or to be kind to the neighbor we consider a jerk or a stranger who is homeless. Yet, we often ask why God did not answer our prayers.

An irony is that the kindness, donations, compassion, behaving well, or committing our lives to serve God is what we have already committed to do as Christians. Another irony is that God is not concerned with giving us what we want to satisfy our selfishness. She is concerned with giving us what we need to live more fully the Christian life portrayed in the Sermon on the Mount.

God knows what is right for us. He knows our wounds and how to heal them. He knows that we need to love Him and others with His love. He knows what is needed in the world and how we can participate with Him to meet the needs of the world.

To know the difference between what we need and what we want is not easy. Jesus said that we have to spend time in silence and solitude to learn what God expects of us to live the Christian life. We have to give the Spirit the time and space to teach us what the world and we need.

Being straight with God is opening our hearts to let the Spirit transform them from what we want it filled with to what God wants it filled with. The Spirit leads us to a new life as we awaken to what we need and surrender to Her will to receive what we need.

Being straight with God comes out of trusting Him. If we want a deeper relationship with God, we let the Spirit teach us to learn and focus on our needs as we learn more how God loves the universe and us.

A Blessing

We are here to trust God's love to give us what we need without our bargaining for what we want. We are here to be in honest relationships with Her and others.

A Prayer

Loving God, I desire to trust your Spirit to lead me to trusting you with my whole heart. I desire to trust You enough to pray simply and honestly for what You know I need.

Chapter 42: Do God's Good for People

"Here is a simple, rule-of-thumb guide for behavior: Ask yourself what you want people to do for you, then grab the initiative and do it for *them*. Add up God's Law and Prophets and this is what you get." (7:12)

What does junior want for Christmas? What should I get Aunt Maude this year for her 80th birthday? What on earth can I possibly get mom and dad for their 40th wedding anniversary that they don't already have?

These are the questions we may ask more often than the one Jesus asks. We tend to focus on what will please a family member or friend so that they are pleased with us and what we gave them. We are concerned receiving praise and knowing that we have please a relative or friend.

If the question Jesus asks is not a familiar one to us, what could he mean? Are we to buy someone a Mercedes because that is what we want? Are we to buy them a season ticket to the local concert series because that is what we want? Are we to buy them a trip to Ireland because we want to go?

I imagine that whoever receives these gifts will be pleased. We may receive a lot of hugs and expressions of gratitude for our gifts. However, I believe that Jesus has different gifts in mind.

Jesus has not been teaching us about giving earthly treasures to others. He pointed out that earthly gifts will be dissolved by rust or thieves might steal them.

He has focused on heavenly treasures that we give to others. He said that heavenly gifts do not rust or can be stolen. Heavenly gifts include faithfulness, love, mercy, goodness, patience and kindness.

Heavenly gifts come from God. They are ready for us now. We have only to desire to receive them through the Spirit. They come into our hearts as God's transforming love.

The purpose of desiring our hearts to be filled with God's love and mercy is that we are being transformed to live in and through Her love. Her love and mercy deepen our relationship with Her and transforms our lives to live in peace, humility, and purity of heart.

We cannot do this alone. There are too many earthly treasures that do not support our faith journey. We need the Spirit to fill our hearts with heavenly gifts.

We know that it is an act of love to give to others what they need. We assume in faith that what everyone needs is the love and mercy that come freely from God. It is already present in our lives waiting for us to desire them.

We do not wait for others to ask us for heavenly gifts. We take the initiative to give heavenly gifts as the Spirit leads and enables us.

Doing for others is an expression of our true self. Our true self from God enables us to show the kingdom of God's love to the world. It enables us to engage in forgiveness and reconciliation. This enables us to work with the Spirit to help all of us to express our true selves, as we give and receive heavenly gifts.

A Blessing

We are here to give acts of love to others the same spontaneous ways as God does.

A Prayer

Generous Christ, I desire your Spirit to lead me into ways giving to others before they give to me.

Chapter 43: No Shortcuts to God

"Don't look for short cuts to God. The market is flooded with surefire, easygoing formulas for a successful life that can be practiced in your spare time. Don't fall for that stuff, even though crowds of people do. The way to life — to God — is vigorous and requires total attention." (7:13-14)

We have glimpses in the Gospels of some of the spiritual life of the Jews in the time of Jesus. Prayer was central. Jews went to the Temple on designated days to offer sacrifices asking God for forgiveness or offering thanksgiving. The people of Israel went to the Temple at Passover to remember their liberation by God from slavery.

They gave tithes and offerings to the Temple as told in the story of the widow's mite. They were to help those in need such as was told in the parable of the Good Samaritan. There are other stories that tell us of spiritual practices.

The life of a believer in Israel was not considered an occasional activity. The Pharisees wrote many other spiritual practices that had developed over the years as traditions. Spiritual practices were daily activity to glorify God and draw closer to Her.

The Christian church continued to follow many of the Jewish spiritual practices. They created some that were appropriate to the new life from God in Christ. The Orthodox and Roman Catholic Churches developed spiritual practices and holy days for people to follow in expressing their piety and as spiritual practices. The churches had worship services called Masses every day that people attended before the start of their day.

Since the days of the advent of Enlightenment into culture in the 1500s, the emphasis on knowledge about God became more prominent in Christian spiritual practices. It was more important to know catechisms and bible verses about God. Not much emphasis was placed on the ancient Christian Contemplative practices.

Jesus and Paul, the mothers and fathers of the deserts, and those practicing the Contemplative Life gave greater emphasis developing a heart to heart relationship with God. In the last 70 years or more many people are recovering Contemplative practices. The leaders of this revival include Fr. Thomas Keating, Fr. Thomas Merton, Fr. Richard, Fr. Basil Pennington, Rev. Dr. Cynthia Bourgeault, and Dr. Jim Finley, who studied under Fr. Thomas Merton.

We are rediscovering through Contemplative practices the importance of being in intimate relationship with God. We are rediscovering that God through thee Spirit is transforming our lives to live God's way, especially in God's love and mercy. We are rediscovering the importance of daily prayer in solitude and silence as Jesus encouraged us, as I reflected in Chapter 27 above.

People today are questioning organized religion because of its rigidity giving more emphasis to the church organization and ideology than showing people the way of intimacy with God through the Contemplative Life. They understand the importance of the emphasis on prayer, bible reading, and other spiritual practices.

However, most of us have busy lives. We have a lot of demands on our time between home, work, children, civic clubs, friends, family, and church. We may not be sure that we can take 20 to 30 minutes out of our day for Centering Prayer or *Lectio Divina*.

This leads us to ask ourselves, how will our hearts be transformed to follow Jesus' command to become one with God and to love God, neighbor, and being loved by God.

In our busy lives it is more convenient and takes less time to learn about God than to spend the time of silence and solitude to develop an intimate relationship with God. Pray may become more of an intellectual conversation than listening for God's word and experience God's presence. God is already present in our lives if we but consent to open our hearts to receive Him.

For many an hour of worship on Sunday is enough. The liturgy is familiar and leaves us primarily with a good feeling. Sermons tell us how we are supposed to live good moral lives. We do our best to be good people and accept that as all that God expects.

People also want to be pious and grow in faith. They are happy to find short cuts through pre-programs prayers and bible study. These pre-program activities become short cuts to let us give honor to God and not require much of our time in living God's love with and for others.

The point of spiritual practices is to surrender our self-centeredness to God and desire the Spirit to transform our lives to live in God's love and mercy. Jesus in his table discourses found in John 14, 15, and 16 said that his disciples are to become one with God as Jesus was one with Her.

Our life in God requires daily spiritual practices of being willing to God's presence in our lives and to desire the Spirit to lead us in the ways of Christ's life. It takes time daily praying in solitude and listening to the Spirit in our heart to experience the transformed life that Jesus called us to follow him in living. There is much in our lives that we must let go that we embraced from culture for our comfort and well-being. Life in God requires total attention because it requires all of our heart, mind, and actions.

We cannot live God's way of life by trying to relate with Him using short cuts. Short cuts would include programed spiritual practices that require no more of us than to read something and briefly pray. Short cuts usually do not require that our lives to be transformed to reveal daily His kingdom.

This is not easy. We have to make the time to be with God and let the Spirit lead us to an intimate relationship with Her. We will need the support and guidance of the Spirit and also the body of brothers and sisters in Christ.

A Blessing

We are here to make the choice of a deeper heart to heart relationship with God. We are here to let the Spirit lead us into living a transformed life based on Her love, mercy, kindness, joy, compassion, gentleness, goodness, generosity, trust, patience, and grace.

A Prayer

My desire is that your Spirit transforms my life to grow ever closer to.

Chapter 44: Look at Leader's Character

"Be wary of false preachers who smile a lot, dripping with practiced sincerity. Chances are they are out to rip you off some way or other. Don't be impressed with charisma; look for character. Who preachers *are* is the main thing, not what they say. A genuine leader will never exploit your emotions or your pocketbook. These diseased trees with their bad apples are going to be chopped down and burned." (7:15-20)

I worked on contract in a church that became enthralled with an interim preacher because he spoke well, he looked good, and he was very personable. I knew this man from daily contact with him as he served as interim pastor for a few months. At the time I was interim associate pastor doing the administrative work at the church.

He was very wounded in his heart from a recent divorce. His wife had left him for another man. He was surprised at her leaving. He had worked for a little while with a therapist.

He did not show his hurt during his time of serving as interim pastor. The people on the search committee did not think the divorce would be a factor in his ministry. Church members in general had the same impression.

Some asked me what I thought. I suggested that his divorce was still too painful and raw for him to serve them at this time. They disagreed with me since they wanted to call him.

I was told that he would get over this and be a good pastor to the congregation. I knew then that I was to say no more. The leaders of the church and most of the congregation had decided to call him.

He had to leave the church for a time according to the denomination's constitution before he could be called as the full time and installed pastor. After the required time the congregation called him.

I left my position even though asked to stay. I knew I could not work with him. Not only was he wounded he also expected to have his way and would accept no other.

About six months after he was called, I was called by the clerk of session. He asked me to talk with this pastor since I knew him. I was told that he was putting too much of his hurts in his sermons. I was told that his sermons were like his talking to a therapist.

The congregation was feeling like the therapist. They wanted the high-quality sermons he had preached when he served as interim.

I had lunch with him. When I brought up the concern, he rationalized that every preacher made personal references in their sermons. I reported this back to the clerk of session of the church.

Several months later he left the church. He went into therapy again. This time he stayed until he felt healed.

Congregations fall into the trap of considering the outward appearance of a person they want to call as pastor. They don't look closely enough at the total character of the persons, which includes events, from which he still felt the wounds

In this case his character was dominated by the deep wounds of the divorce and the negative self-image he felt from it. The church did not see how deeply hurt his heart and mind was. They did not want to look at the affect his divorce and heart-wound would affect his ministry.

I believe the emphasis of Jesus in this passage is on the love and mercy in a pastor's heart. The pastor is to produce the fruits of God's love and mercy in ways that are obvious. The pastor is to be a servant of the people and not insistent on her or his own way.

I learned this in a very painful way. I went into a church full of conflict that members and leaders conspired to ignore. When I pointed it out, my ministry became a two-year interim with my leaving after the two years. It took the church another 4 years to transform from a family run church to a church that included all the members in decisions and the life of the church.

An important question is what is more important for a pastor: the needs of the people or her or his needs. This can be discerned by how quickly, if at all, he or she turns the conversation to himself or herself.

Another important character indicator is how much time the prospective pastor spends in spiritual practices. Another indicator is asking his references how he showed love, compassion, and leadership. Another indicator is what he or she would expect to do at the church during the first year. This latter would indicate whether the pastor is more concerned with the church or with his agenda.

I have tried to indicate how important is the character of the pastor. Her or his character is not different from the character a church would expect of anyone in a leadership position. Actually, the characteristics are to be the same in all members.

I have known churches that have elected men and women to official boards without asking about the character of the potential nominee. Most nominating committees have expressed relief that someone would agree to serve.

The question Jesus raises is what fruits of the Spirit is most visible in a pastor's life. These fruits include: love, compassion, kindness, friendship, trustworthiness, goodness, generosity, prayer, and patience. These are some of the fruits a church member in leadership position and a pastor need to produce, to help all members to produce the same fruits.

My experience is that the character of the pastor and other leaders in a church reflects and influences the character of the church.

A Blessing
Pastors and church leaders are to open their hearts to let the Spirit to enable them to produce the character traits (fruits) of God's love. All Christians are called to produce these fruits and, especially, to take advantage of no one.

A Prayer
Loving Christ, open our hearts and minds to listen and to look for your fruits of character, particularly as pastors and leaders.

Chapter 45: Missing the Boat

"Knowing the correct password—saying 'Master, Master,' for instances—isn't going to get you anywhere with me. What is required is serious obedience—*doing* what my Father wills. I can see it now—at the Final Judgment thousands strutting up to me and saying, 'Master, we preached the Message, we bashed the demons, our God-sponsored projects had everyone talking.' And do you know what I am going to say? 'You missed the boat. All you did was use me to make you important. You don't impress me one bit. You're out of here." (7:21-23)

Jesus has led us to this passage from the first verse of Matthew 5. He has said in a variety of ways what it means to live a Christian life. As we have worked our way through these three chapters, we have read some ways of faith living that many people find difficult to think of much less asking God to transform them to live that way. I have tried to highlight these expectations that Christ has for Christians as individuals and a community of faith his teachings on being the kingdom of God on earth.

The Christian life is about relationships and actions. It is based on God's way of seeing people through His love and mercy. Living the Christian life requires that we look to the Spirit to guide us in the Christian life since we are tempted by sin to place having power, wealth, esteem, and entitlement first in our lives. The Spirit spends our lifetime filling our hearts with God's way when we desire the presence of God by opening our hearts to the work of the Spirit. This transforms us to increase in our love relationship with God and revealing as individuals and a community of Christ to the whole world.

In this passage Jesus imagines at the end of time what many people claiming to be his followers will approach him. He imagines that they will come bragging about all that they have done to save the lost and to defeat the devil. They want Jesus to know how hard that they have worked developing soul-winning programs in his name. He assumes that these people will tell him all the programs and great works they had done for him and God.

Jesus uses three particular metaphors, or imagines, that stand out for me. One metaphor is 'strutting.' We know about strutting. That is how some people walk when they are proud of what they have done or are doing.

Marching bands strut because they are proud of their school and how well they perform as a band. You can see the drum major strutting to entertain people watching and because he or she is proud of the band. Some bands strut in their marching to entertain the on-lookers as part of the rhythm of their playing.

Another image or metaphor in the passage that stands out is 'bashing.' People tell Jesus that they have bashed demons. We know that bashing is the act of using something to crush a person to death usually. The people are describing to Christ what <u>they</u> did in bashing demons. They are expecting Christ to believe that they have bashed a power greater than their own. They have not asked for God's help, which is the only power strong enough to "bash" the devils.

The third image, or metaphor, seems more positive. It is an image of putting on church programs that would bring many people to God. I imagine that they are bragging to Jesus about their soul winning and other programs.

The people who appear before Jesus on judgment day are proud of their programs. They are proud that the programs attracted church members and non-members. They are proud of all they believe that they accomplished.

The three metaphors are intended to draw attention to what these followers of Jesus have done for him. They describe their performances to impress the community with the work of God. They also want to impress God with all that they had done for Her.

The people focus spotlights on their performances. They are likely anticipating applause for their work. They are expecting praise from God and Christ for all the demons smashed and the people saved through their efforts.

Jesus made several points in Matthew 6 that we can expect silence from Heaven for our performances. The people Jesus is speaking of are describing how well they performed as Christians. Jesus says that God does not applaud our performances.

This may surprise us because we are doing all this work for God. However, Jesus says that performances are not what God is looking for. God is not looking for how well we bashed demons or put on impressive evangelistic programs. This is our little ego wanting to make an impression to receive all the heavenly treasures that God will give.

God is looking for humility in living His kingdom. He expects us to do our work guided by the Spirit in His love and mercy. He is looking for humility that asks for no credit or desires earthly treasures or other rewards.

Jesus says that all of these programs and efforts miss the boat with God. What could Jesus mean by missing the boat when we have been so successful in doing God's work?

We have missed the boat of having our lives changed by the work of the Spirit. The boat we miss with God is opening our hearts to have a deeper heart to heart relationship with Her. It is the boat of giving Her love to others daily.

We miss the boat when we emphasize our good works. These are the works we have been told through the centuries are important to make God proud of us. We may forget that our works are of God and an expression of God's love.

Before Jesus, the prophet Micah wrote in 6:8, 'It's quite simple: Do what is fair and just to your neighbor, be compassionate and loyal in your love, and don't take yourself too seriously—take God seriously.' It is about relationships based in God's love and mercy.

We catch the boat when we open our hearts to an intimate relationship with God. It is a relationship that is founded on the rock of His love and mercy for us. It is a heart to heart relationship with Him based on His love that transforms our lives to live the spiritual gifts Paul listed in Galatians 5:22-23 and Jesus gave us as the Beatitudes. Out of these come the love we give to others that enable them also to catch the boat to which the Spirit is leading us.

A Blessing
God wants a loving relationship with us rather than programs that encourage others to give us words of praise or to give us applause.

A Prayer
Loving and merciful God, Thank you for the Spirit who teaches me to be part of your work of love and to let go of my ego looking for applause.

Chapter 46: Living on the Solid Rock

"These words I speak to you are not incidental additions to your life, homeowners' improvements to your standard of living. They are foundational words, words to build a life on. If you work these words into your life, you are like a smart carpenter who builds his house on solid rock. Rain poured down, the river flooded, a tornado hit—but nothing moved that house. It was fixed to the rock. "But if you just use my words in Bible studies and don't work them into your life, you are like a stupid carpenter who built his house on the sandy beach. When a storm rolled in and the waves came up, it collapsed like a house of cards."
(7:24-27)

Looking back over my life I find this passage very applicable. In general, I believe the passage is another way to say what is needed for a solid foundation of our Christian life.

The Spirit has awakened me to how little I have known in the past about God's love and mercy. I am awakened even more to how little I have lived His love during my life.

It is not that I have not loved. It is that my loving has been more an expression of my little ego than the gratuitous love that God has given me.

I had three events in my life that have opened my heart to consent to the Spirit's lead me to the rock upon which to build my house of faith. They continue to be used by the Spirit to guide me to God's love and my true self.

I thought at the time that I was living God's love. Occasionally I actually did. However, the love that I had identified as Hers was not the rock foundation of life that the Spirit is awakened to me now.

With that introduction I have a true story somewhat disguised about my second conversion, as St Therese of Lisieux named her experience. It is a story that illustrates for me the parable in this passage.

As I said above, I have had three major events in my life that have been transforming. The first was being asked to leave a church and my wife left me at the same time. I know my contribution to these events. However, the being asked to leave was unexpected.

I felt as if I was sitting in the midst of my collapsed life's house. The only part of the house that remained was the foundation.

It took me a while to recognize that the foundation was God's love and mercy. Unfortunately, the recognition was more intellectual than life transforming.

Awakening to that reality opened my eyes to a new path that God was offering me. She was giving me the opportunity to walk a different way and walk a different journey.

I've walked that journey as best I could. I have come to realize how much I need the Spirit daily to lead me in this new way.

The Spirit began to show me the depth and breadth of God's love and mercy. I knew I needed to trust both of these graces as already present from God.

My house of faith and life collapsing around me has become the image of my building my house on sand. It was made out of material that my ego collected and my false self said was good enough. Both of these had more to do with what I wanted, or thought was right. The foundation and the building materials proved weak when the storm occurred at the church and in my marriage.

After that first event, I was awakened to the need to surrender my will to God's will. This prepared me for the second event that showed me I had not surrendered my will as much as I thought I had.

I tried for several years to find how to live with a chronic illness. I did not look often to God or the Spirit for help. I was not successful in finding healing until I surrendered my will and became more regular in my practice of Centering Prayer. After a while the Spirit lead me to give my weakness to God.

A third event awakened me to God's love. I became aware in my heart that God is present and loving me as I am. Until that day I had assumed I knew God's love. After the crisis mentioned above, I came to realize that I knew *about* God's love in my mind. Even now, the Spirit struggles with me to guide me to consenting to God's love displacing the ways of the world slowly but surely. Like everyone I have days that I am open to God's presence and days that I close my heart to God by trying to live by my will.

The Spirit also made me aware in my heart that I am loveable. I began to see as a reality that others love me. The Spirit said to my heart that there is a Page worth knowing inside.

The three events are related. They happened at the times the Spirit knew I was ready to hear and to be transformed. The Spirit showed me that I had built my faith on sand with inferior material. I knew then I needed to let the Spirit lead me to the solid rock and use the materials of God's love and mercy.

Jesus said that he is not describing a remodeling project. He is describing a complete new house, in which to live. This new house can also be described as a new way of life—a house built on the solid foundation of God's love and grace. The Spirit is working with me to build a different house of faith.

The Spirit is showing me how to live simply and honestly in a house built on the foundation of God's love. This rock foundation is strong enough to withstand the chaos and storms that enter my mind and heart. The foundation of Her love will not crack.

I weep at memories of times that I did not share God's love relating with others and myself. These were times that that I was controlled by my little ego wanting its selfish ways. I am grateful for the Spirit for leading me to surrender my will to God's will and to willingly live His way of life.

A Blessing

We are here to let God build our life-house of faith on the foundation of Her love. We are here to let the Spirit instruct us in build a new house of faith and life. We are here willingly to live in Her way, truth, and life revealed in Christ.

Prayer

Gracious and loving God, I feel humble that you are present in my heart to lead me to rebuild my life-house on your foundation of love and mercy.

Chapter 47: An Ending and Beginning

"When Jesus concluded his address, the crowd burst into applause. They had never heard teaching like this. It was apparent that he was living everything he was saying—quite a contrast to their religion teachers! This was the best teaching they had ever heard." (7:28-29)

The crowd had never heard such a moving presentation before. It was given with the sincerity and honesty that they had not heard from the Temple priests. To them it may have been similar to our hearing an inspiriting sermon that stirs our souls.

The crowd could not restrain itself. They knew he lived what he taught. They were so moved by what Jesus said that they burst into applause. They probably gave him a standing ovation.

If this had been a crowd today Jesus probably would have heard a few "bravos" in addition to applause. Some would have crowded around him to shake his hand and pat him on the back. Some would have spoken words of admiration. Others would have thanked him for being so inspiring. Some would have asked for his autograph.

I imagine Jesus' reaction to the applause is to walk away. I imagine that he is sad that they were impressed with him as a speaker more than with the new life message he brought from God. I imagine he knew that some in the crowd might listen to him in the future, but it was not up to him whether they opened their hearts to God's love and to living a transformed life in the Spirit.

He had not tried to outdo the teachings of the Scribes and Pharisees. He was telling people of a new life for them in the heart of God. He was saying the lives of his hearers could be more than they could ask for or imagine if they would surrender to Her will of love and mercy. He was saying to living as he lived and to walk his talk.

The crowd probably did as we do in similar situations. The people left the meeting recounting what they heard and what thrilled them.

Jesus says that it is not words, traditions, or Temple worship that God wants from us. God wants us to live the faith not simply keep it as sets of beliefs, rituals, or traditions. He wants transformed lives of self-emptying of egocentric behaviors and thoughts. He invites us to open their hearts to the life God created us to have.

This passage brings us to the end of the Sermon on the Mount. Jesus presents the purpose of the Sermon in 7:24-27 when he says that the Sermon is about a new life. His teachings are not incidental to our lives.

He tells us that in order to be his followers we have to do more than memorize his teachings and read the Bible. His message is about God's Spirit transforming our lives without consent.

The teachings of Jesus in the Sermon are to be life transforming. They provide the foundation for a new life in Christ. They provide the building material that God gives us to build our life/house in which She and we can dwell together in Her love. The Sermon tells us about living the ways of His kingdom on earth as it is in heaven.

Are we ready to open our hearts completely to God? Are we ready make life in Christ the sole purpose of our lives? Are we ready to let the Spirit guide us in living daily the love and mercy that God gives to us? Are we ready to let the Spirit fill our hearts with God's love and let this love guide all we do and say?

That is all we need to do: to let the Spirit guide us in a new life. We don't have to live the new life perfectly from the beginning. We only need to be willing to let the Spirit lead us on the journey of faith that transforms our lives to live in

God's love and mercy. We travel the path that enables us to give the love and mercy of God's kingdom daily.

As Jesus often said or implied, it is not what we know but whom we are in God's love that matters.

A Blessing

We are here to commit to living the teachings of Jesus and be transformed by God's love and mercy to empty our lives of the ways of earth. We are not here to give Jesus a standing ovation as if he has given us a magnificent entertainment.

A Prayer

O Christ, I desire to open my heart to you to have my life transformed by your way of self-emptying. I desire your Spirit to lead me to learn each day how to live the new life you give me. Teach me how to live your way and truth. Teach me how to walk the talk.

A BENEDICTION

The following entered my heart 50 years ago and has been part of the new life that the Spirit is giving me.

II Corinthians 5:16-20:

"Because of this decision we don't evaluate people by what they have or how they look. We looked at the Messiah that way once and got it all wrong, as you know. We certainly don't look at him that way anymore. Now we look inside, and what we see is that anyone united with the Messiah gets a fresh start, is created new. The old life is gone; a new life burgeons! Look at it! All this comes from the God who settled the relationships with each other. God put the world square with himself through the Messiah, giving the world a fresh start by offering forgiveness of sins. God has given us the task of telling everyone what he is doing. We're Christ's representatives. God uses us to persuade men and women to drop their differences and enter into God's work of making things right between them. We're speaking for Christ himself now: Become friends with God he's already a friend with you."

In the past couple of years, the following passage has joined the above in opening my heart to God:

Philippians 2:6-7: "[Christ] had equal status with God but didn't think so much of himself that he want to cling to the advantages of that status no matter what. Not at all. When the time came he set asked the privileges of deity and took on the status of a slave, became human!"

May you find the words of Christ that guide your lives and give you the foundation upon which to let the Spirit work with you in building your faith house of love and mercy.

THE END and THE BEGINNING

Thank you for sharing this faith journey with me. I pray that you experienced the Spirit in your heart filling it with God's love. I pray that this is the beginning for some and for others the opening of your heart to the Spirit to make you more aware of God's presence. I pray that you may have had times of oneness with God whether for a few seconds or longer. I pray that the Spirit opened your heart and mind to God's love that you may have a deeper glimpse of who God's created you to be.

May you have days in which you experience blessings that transform you to live Christ's loving way. I pray that you may have days that you share God's transforming love to others.

Amen! Amen!

A Brief Biography

Dr. Shelton is an honorably retired PC-USA minister. He has a B.A. degree from Duke University from 1963, as well as a Master of Divinity from Duke Divinity School from 1966. He earned a Doctor of Ministry from Columbia Theological Seminary in Decatur, Georgia in 1985. He has worked in an administrative capacity in the inner city of Charlotte. He has served three churches.

Dr. Shelton also has a Master of Social Work from the University of North Carolina School of School Work from 1975 with a concentration in Organizational Development and Training. He has worked in a county depart of social services; area mental health center; and state coordinator of child protective services. In 2003 he was diagnosed with Fibromyalgia. He chose to retire at that time.

Dr. Shelton has spent over 20 years reading about The Contemplative Life. He has read from the writings of the Desert Fathers and Mothers and contemporary writers in the Contemplative Life. He has committed his life to the daily discipline of Centering Prayer.

He began writing in 2001 on the Sermon on the Mount to gain deeper understand of the Christian life as described by Christ in these three chapters of Matthew's Gospel. That book was published in 2007.

He has also written a trilogy of meditation books. All of his writings are personal reflection on God's presence and love in his life. He has written primarily for his own spiritual journey.

He was encouraged to share his reflections with others. He agreed. He is publishing 3 volumes in three consecutive years. The books are intended to share his journey and support others in their journey.